KU-469-443

# DUTCH UNCLE

by

## SIMON GRAY

FABER AND FABER
24 Russell Square
London

First published in 1969
by Faber and Faber Limited
24 Russell Square London WC1
Printed in Great Britain by
Latimer Trend & Co Ltd Plymouth
All rights reserved

SBN (cloth edition) 571 09015 X
SBN (paper edition) 571 09016 8

© 1969 by Simon Gray

X058854

6/2/69

822.91
Gra

QUEEN MARGARET UNIVERSITY COLLEGE
LEITH CAMPUS LIBRARY

―――――

Please return book by date stamped below

QUEEN MARGARET COLLEGE

100 094 446

QUEEN MARGARET COLLEGE LIBRARY

# CAST

Inspector Hawkins

Police Constable Hedderley

Mr. Godboy

May Godboy

Doris Hoyden

Eric Hoyden

Performing rights for DUTCH UNCLE

All professional and amateur rights in this play are strictly reserved and applications for permission to perform it must be made in advance to Clive Goodwin Associates, 79 Cromwell Road, London SW7

# ACT ONE

## Scene 1

*The year is 1952. A living-room in a decaying house in Shepherd's Bush. The wall, right, (the audience's right, that is) has a door leading into the hall. The wall, left, has a door leading into the bedroom. The back wall, left, has a door that leads into the kitchen. There is a door in the kitchen that also leads into the hall, but is not visible to the audience. Parts of the kitchen—the stove, sink, and parts of the hall —a door, opposite, that leads into the lavatory—are, however, visible to the audience when the appropriate doors are open.*

*The furniture is as follows. Back stage, centre, a shabby sofa. An armchair to the right of it and slightly forward. Two hard-backed utility chairs, one left of sofa, one well away from the armchair and in front of it. On a small table, left, and close to the bedroom door is a gramophone and a pile of records. In the right corner of the room there is an enormous wardrobe, sticking out and carelessly placed. It is tall and deep, freshly varnished and covered with curlicues, etc. Next to it, against the wall and to the left, is a more conventional wardrobe, shallower and slimmer. Both wardrobes have drawers in their bases. On the other side of the enormous wardrobe and to its right, against the wall and close to the door that leads to the hall, is an alcove covered by two curtains that don't quite meet and don't quite reach the ground. The heels of shoes and a few inches of boxes are therefore visible, also sleeves of jackets, etc. The room is very messy. Bits of newspapers and women's magazines scattered about, a pair of woman's high-heeled shoes near the gramophone table, two empty packets of cigarettes on one of the utility chairs.*

*The curtain rises on the room, empty. There is a long silence, then a slight thumping noise from the large cupboard. The door opens and* MR. GODBOY *steps out. He is carrying a gas cylinder with a length of rubber tubing, very long, attached to its nozzle. He puts this into the alcove, hangs the rubber tubing so that it sticks out a fraction from between the curtain, goes to the door, looks casually around the*

7

*room, then walks forward very quickly. With his left hand he slams
the door shut, with his right hand he seizes the length of tubing,
plunges it into a hole on the right side of the cupboard, then pulling
the cylinder out, pretends to turn the nozzle with his right hand.
Takes the tube out, puts it back as before, puts the cylinder back
behind the alcove curtain, unlocks the cupboard door. Takes out of
his coat pocket an enormous padlock, shut, with the key in it.
Checks the padlock against the bolt, then holding the padlock, opens
the cupboard door, steps inside, out of view, shuts the door behind
him. Bangs on the cupboard door. The noises are muffled. Stops.
There is a short silence then the door, right, opens and* MAY GODBOY
*comes in. She is wearing a baggy dress and flattened shoes and an
overcoat. She is carrying a basket with a greasy package on top. She
puts the basket down, bends over it. While she is doing this the cupboard door opens a fraction.* MAY *stiffens, turns, stares at the cupboard, puts her hands on her hips in amazement. Then the door opens
wide and* MR GODBOY *steps out, falters a fraction of an instant. The
padlock, closed, is in his right hand. He closes the door fussily,
keeping the padlock out of sight.*

GODBOY: Oh hello dear, I wasn't expecting you for another
    hour, you said.
MAY: What's that?
GODBOY (*slipping the padlock into his right jacket pocket, drops
    it to the floor, picks it up with a*): Whoops! (*Laughs.*) It's a
    cupboard, dear.
MAY (*still staring at the cupboard*): What's it doing in here?
GODBOY: Oh no dear (*stuffing the padlock into his pocket*), it's
    not for us (*laughs*), it's for Eric and Doris. (*Little pause.*)
    As cupboard space was conditional on acceptance of terms
    for the upstairs apartment, legally furnishings have to be
    approved as adequate.
MAY: Who by?
GODBOY: Um, Eric and Doris that would be, dear.
MAY: And have they come complaining?
GODBOY: It's a matter of conscience also, dear.
MAY: Whose?
GODBOY: Mine, that would be, dear.

MAY: If it's for Eric and Doris, what's it doing down here?

GODBOY: It's merely for the time being, dear.

MAY (*looks at him, turns, picks up the basket, turns again*): And what was you doing inside it then?

GODBOY: Investigating it for capacity, dear, merely. (*Long pause.*) Would you like to have a look-see? (*Opens the cupboard door, makes a formal ushering gesture.*)

(MAY *walks closer to it, stares in suspiciously. As she does so* MR. GODBOY'*s right hand moves from the pipe hanging out of the alcove.*)

MAY: What for?

GODBOY: It's very capacious, dear.

MAY: Perhaps it is.

(*She steps away.* MR. GODBOY *drops his hand.*)

But that doesn't mean I have to live in it. (*Walks across to the sofa, settles on it, takes off her coat, flings it on to the utility chair. It slides off, falls to the floor.*) What do you think I am, some class of hermit? (*Chuckles.*) Because no I'm not, no I'm not. (*She stares at him significantly.*)

GODBOY (*comes over, picks up her coat, folds it over the back of the chair*): Well dear, to tell you the truth, I've already been and placed some of your garments inside it. Your nightie and a frock you're fond of plus your comfy carpet slippers, dear, and other odds and ends.

MAY: Why?

GODBOY: Well, I thought we'd avail ourselves of the use of it, while we had it. Legally it's our cupboard until it's theirs. (*Looks at her.*) Anyway, if there's any article you can't find, it's likely to be in the cupboard waiting for you, you could peer in now for a check.

(MAY *swings her legs up on to the sofa.*)

But if I'm not here, give me a call so I can help you sort through. . . .

MAY: Ooo, the headaches you give me, you make a fuss out of breathing.

(GODBOY *goes back to the cupboard, shuts the door, turns to the guppie case, scatters food from a packet into it.*)

GODBOY: I'm sorry, dear, it was just a little idea of mine.

9

(MAY *reaches down to the basket, picks the package up, opens it. It contains chips. She begins to pop them into her mouth.* MR. GODBOY *turns, stares. She stares back at him, goes on eating.*)

GODBOY: Tasty?

MAY: Is that what you been doing all afternoon, then?

GODBOY (*smiling*): Pardon, dear?

MAY: Messing about with cupboards?

GODBOY: Yes dear.

MAY (*knowing*): You sure?

GODBOY: There was a lot to be looked after dear. It had to be purchased first, then arrangements had to be made for its delivery, myself accompanying in the van, no laughing matter as you can imagine, then various matters arose in connection with the padlock I insisted on for security measures. . . .

(*He hesitates, then boldly takes the padlock out of his pocket, flashes it at her, stuffs it away. While he is talking,* MAY *gets off the sofa and goes into the kitchen, leaving the door open.* MR. GODBOY *hurries over to the sofa, picks up her coat, takes it to the cupboard, puts it in, shuts the door, as* MAY *comes back in, sprinkling vinegar over her chips.*)

GODBOY (*coming back to the centre of the room*): And on top of that I had to supervise the placing of the cupboard, also no laughing——

MAY: Doris or Eric didn't drop down then?

GODBOY: No dear, as I was explaining, I was compelled to be out all afternoon.

MAY: Well, Eric was down looking for you while you was gadding about with cupboards; he wants to know when you're going to do some work on his Doris, if you're still up to doing work on anyone, that is . . . (*settling back on the sofa*) seeing as he says as he's asked you five times.

GODBOY (*after a pause*): Yes dear, it's been a matter of waiting until the time is right, which it now is.

MAY: And there I was thinking you'd be glad to get your hands on her shy little toes; think of the liberties (*making prising gesture with a chip*) while you was knocking off a corn.

10

(MR. GODBOY *looks at her, then goes to the kitchen door, shuts it, comes back, sits down on one of the utility chairs, laughs, shakes his head.*)

GODBOY: I hope you don't joke like that around the neighbourhood, dear, on account of what you know it could do in the way of damage to my professional standing.

MAY (*sucks her fingers*): Oh and would it? (*Wags her head.*) What standing?

GODBOY: It might give people the unfortunate impression that everything wasn't right between us, dear.

MAY: It's unfortunate where the truth is, then. (*Pause.*) What about the standing that never stands because it's already had damage done to it according to your story and as I was the last to know?

GODBOY (*after a long pause*): Pardon, dear?

MAY: I've been thinking. How's your wound today? Throbbing, is it? Throbbing away?

GODBOY: It's merely been causing me a trifling pain, dear, thank you for asking. I managed to get down to the chemist for a prescription refill that'll assist me to doze off at night.

MAY (*sarcastic*): Well, that'll bring me some peace at last, won't it. (*Little pause.*) Your passion's been on the doze since the day we was married. (*Gets up, looks irritably around the room.*) And so's your foot-doctoring, so's your everything.

GODBOY (*watching her alertly*): As you know dear—are you looking for something?

MAY: Where's my coat?

GODBOY: I popped it in the cupboard. (*Gesturing towards it.*) I believe it would be fatal for me to practise full time owing to the effect on my pension and side-benefits, even my little family legacy would suffer.

(*As* MAY *goes towards the cupboard, he gets out of his chair.*) And the fact that I'm perfectly willing to assist out on the wife of a tenant doesn't mean I have to go begging for it, merely, dear.

(*Sits down again as* MAY *walks past the cupboard to the alcove, pulls the curtain back, heaves the cylinder out of the way, scrambles about on a shelf, knocking down bits and*

11

*pieces of clothes, then comes back wiping her hands on a
large handkerchief.* MAY *blows her nose, settles back on the
sofa as* MR. GODBOY *goes to the alcove, puts the cylinder right
while pretending to be putting the clothes back.*)

MAY: What's that?

GODBOY: Pardon, dear?

MAY: Those tubes and pipes?

GODBOY: Oh. (*Laughs.*) Merely a little device I was offered at
the chemist to try out a little experiment with merely, dear.
(*Straightening, he closes the curtain.*)

MAY (*looking at him*): All day I've been thinking about you. I've
got a surprise coming up for you.

GODBOY: Pardon, dear? (*brushing at his clothes*).

MAY: When we got started together you was brim-full of talk
about how you was going to swell up until you was too big
to handle on your own, as feet was feet and would always
cause pain and need doctoring, and all I seen you do in
two years of marriage is monkey about on that pension of
yours and go on about your wound and bother them down
at the police station. (*Points a finger at him as he comes
back.*) Where else was you this afternoon? (*Nods.*) Where
was you? At the police station, that's where you was,
wasn't you?

GODBOY (*sits down*): Indeed, dear, I did drop in for a chat this
morning.

MAY (*kicks off her shoes, sighs*): And what was you doing down
there this time?

GODBOY: Merely discussing, dear, as I said.

MAY: What?

GODBOY (*after a pause*): Murder, merely, dear.

MAY: What murder?

GODBOY: James Ryan O'Higgs, the Dublin accountant and wife
and female tenant murderer, dear. The one who polished
off his wife and tenant in a week, and how he kept the
police at bay with clever lies, although they was—were
suspicious after the first. But still he kept on at it. . . .
(*As* MAY *gets up, he watches her.*)
Chat merely, dear.

(*Getting to his feet as* MAY *goes to the cupboard.*)
What you might call shop.
(*Moving towards her as she opens the cupboard door: takes the padlock out of his pocket.* MAY *turns, looks at him. He has been walking furtively, now walks nonchalantly to stand beside her.*)

MAY (*looks at him with contempt*): No wonder you need medicine, the way you fill your brain up with stuff like that.
(*She moves closer to the cupboard as* MR. GODBOY *slips behind her to the alcove.*)
Where did you say my slippers was?
(*He puts his hand against the cupboard door to shut it, takes the pipe in his right hand. He cannot of course see* MAY, *as the cupboard door blocks her from view.*)

GODBOY: That's right dear, in there dear.
(MAY *steps around from the cupboard, stands behind* MR. GODBOY, *who is still poised, holding the pipe in his right, the door in his left hand.*)
He did it by gassing, May! (*in a shout*).
(*He slams the door as* MAY *puts a hand on his shoulder. He whirls around, laughs.*)

MAY (*as* MR. GODBOY *drops the pipe*): What's the matter with you, I don't care if he did it by eating them raw; let me through and why can't you leave my things alone.
(*As* MR. GODBOY *steps away from the alcove, she bends down, knocking aside the cylinder, then comes out carrying a pair of slippers.*)

GODBOY: Those are mine, dear. Yours are in the cupboard.

MAY: They'll suit.
(*She puts them on. He watches her malevolently.*)
And talking of gas, you be careful; the number of times you left the oven taps on for no reason, it's a wonder you're still here. And now it's tubes and what.

GODBOY (*laughs*): Merely a device. . . . (*Slips the padlock back in his pocket.*)

MAY (*turning her back on him*): Not that it matters. I've got a surprise for you.

GODBOY: Indeed? What sort of surprise?

MAY: You'll find out when it comes. (*She settles again on the sofa.*) And who was you having this chat with? Your Inspector Hawkins?

GODBOY: With Duty Officer Larkins, dear. (*Shuts the door, comes back.*) Although it's funny you should mention Inspector Hawkins, dear, as he did come in while I was talking to Duty Officer.

MAY: And has he remembered you yet?

GODBOY: His eyes were red-rimmed with fatigue and there was stubble on his chin; I garnered from Duty Officer's hints that he's been working twenty-four hours on the Merrit Street case—he wasn't in a condition to remember me.

MAY: But he's been at that station two months now, and you been down there every day of the week, how is it he don't remember you if you was so close to him in the war?

GODBOY (*stiffly*): I never said I expected him to remember me, May, I merely said in my capacity as Special Constable we'd come into contact before he was posted.

MAY: Ooooh! Well, to hear you tell it sometimes, you was always at his side.

GODBOY: I admire him May, yes, and I've followed his career, yes, and I'm proud to have been in contact, yes, and that's all I've said May.

MAY: And yet he don't remember you even! Yes?

GODBOY (*looks at her coldly*): Inspector Hawkins will remember me all right, May, when the time comes.

MAY (*stares at him*): It's funny to me the way your voice changes at the mention of his name, why didn't you marry him instead.

(*Long pause.* MR. GODBOY *is sitting stiffly.*)

And from what I hear you're not the only one's coming into contact with Hawkins. Who was he with?

GODBOY (*coldly*): Pardon?

MAY: Who was your Hawkins with?

GODBOY: He was in the company of a female constable.

MAY: That sounds like the Hawkins I've been hearing about.

GODBOY (*still coldly*): Doubtless she has a key part to play in the Merrit Street case, May, given the nature of the offence.

14

MAY: As long as she's female that's not all she'll have a key
part to play in, constable or no constable, from what they
say about Hawkins.

GODBOY (*after a little pause*): There's always gossip about
inspectors of a filthy nature.

MAY: Oh, he's of a filthy nature all right, ladies and Hawkins
are never out of each other's sight, that's what I hear.

GODBOY: You're talking about Inspector Hawkins, May. There's
not, nor never has been no stain on his record.

MAY: That's not where the stains would be. Manly Hawkins!
(MR. GODBOY *sits staring straight ahead.*)

MAY: Isn't that what they call him?

GODBOY: That nickname was acquired because he's got the
looks and manners of a born policeman. At first it was
Irish Hawkins, but he soon put a stop to that, and then it
was Mannerly Hawkins, from the respect he'd earned with
his politeness, and then people got careless with it and it
slipped into Manly, which only a few proven constables
ever called him by to his face and was—were allowed to get
away with it in my hearing, if he thought highly of them to
be on intimate returns. (*Little pause.*) As for the female
constable, if she's working under Inspector Hawkins, and
has been brought in special to do it, it's because she's
developed a reputation in her own right. (*Little pause.*) I'm
under oath to Duty Officer not to divulge what she's been
requested to do in the Merrit Street case, I can only say
she's in danger up to the hilt.

MAY (*laughs tauntingly*): If she's hanging about hoping the
Merrit Street attacker will rip off her skirts to get in her up
to the hilt, then that's Hawkins's idea of pleasure too, from
what I hear, oh yes what the Merrit Street attacker don't
give her, Hawkins'll make up for.
(*Long pause.* MR. GODBOY *sits staring straight ahead.*)
And I'll tell *you* something, I wouldn't mind being in her
shoes. With *either* of them.

GODBOY: May I ask, May, may I ask where this gossip you've
been hearing's been taking place?

MAY: Never you mind where.

15

GODBOY: Because I don't believe you've had the pleasure of seeing Inspector Hawkins in the flesh.

MAY: And he hasn't had the pleasure of seeing me the same way. (*Laughs.*) It's a wonder to me they let you come snooping around the station, you've got no business there, and as for Manly Hawkins, he'd order you back to the corns and bunions, which is where you belong, if he noticed you at all, which he won't.

GODBOY (*laughs softly*): He'll notice me, May, when the time comes.

MAY: Well, I won't be here to see it. (*Significantly picks up and shakes the cigarette packs.*)

(MR. GODBOY *looks at her, looks away.*)

MAY: And you remember I said that. (*Little pause, feeling irritably under her.*) Where's my coat then?

GODBOY: Oh, I do believe I hung it in the new cupboard, dear. (MAY *sighs, gets up, tramps across the room to the cupboard.*)

MAY: I have to do everything for myself in the place, why can't you leave me alone?

(*As* MR. GODBOY *follows her. She opens the cupboard, stands thinking as* MR. GODBOY *comes up behind her, then leaving the door open, goes out of the hall door, right, leaving that open also.* MR. GODBOY *is fumbling for the padlock.*)

GODBOY: No dear (*laughs*), it's in the cupboard here. (*Shakes his fist, then goes out into the hall after her. As he does so the door, left, opens, and* MAY *comes tramping in holding some cigarettes and matches, lights up as she settles back on the sofa.* MR. GODBOY *reappears through the kitchen door.*)

MAY: What you doing, following me about like a mongolese idiot?

GODBOY: I thought you wanted your coat, which is in the cupboard dear. (*Shuts the kitchen door, comes over to his chair, sits down.*)

MAY: What for? Im not going anywhere—yet. It was me fags I wanted. (*Taps ash on the floor.*)

(MR. GODBOY *sits staring at her. After a minute gets up, picks up an ashtray from the gramophone table, puts it on*

16

*the floor beside her, makes to sit down, then goes across,*
*makes to shut the cupboard door, looks quickly at* MAY,
*leaves it open and shuts the hall door. Comes back. Sits down.*
*There is a silence.*

MAY: My number one would have laughed, he hated the police.

GODBOY: I know he did, dear, but your first husband and myself
was—were comparatively speaking two different kettles of
fish.

MAY: Yes he was.

*(She draws on the cigarette, reaches down, stubs it out on the*
*floor beside the ashtray without looking.* MR. GODBOY *watches,*
*then goes across, picks up the butt, puts it in the tray.* MAY
*watches him.)*

MAY: He enjoyed himself, that one did. For one thing he liked
good-bye parties.

GODBOY *(sitting down)*: Pardon dear?

MAY: Nothing. I've got a shock in store for you, that's all. And
the first of it is that Eric and Doris is coming down later.

GODBOY *(after a pause)*: Eric and Doris dear? *(In a controlled*
*voice.)* Indeed? Tonight dear?

MAY: That's right, but I'm not telling you why, because it's got
pleasure in it, and you don't know what that is.

*(MR. GODBOY *after another pause, gets up, walks over to the*
*cupboard door.)*

GODBOY: I was under the impression we was—were having a
quiet night all by ourselves, dear. *(He shuts the cupboard*
*door, comes back.)*

MAY: Was you? *(Points to the cupboard.)* Clear it out.

GODBOY *(sitting down)*: Pardon, dear?

MAY: Clear it out. Kindly clean that cupboard out of my things,
Number Two. *(Claps her hands.)* That you been kind
enough to fill it up with. I'm going to be needing them
later.

GODBOY: I don't understand dear.

MAY: You will soon enough.

*(There is a long pause.* MAY *claps her hands again.* MR
GODBOY *gets to his feet, walks to the cupboard. Stops before*
*it.)*

GODBOY: You want me to get your things out, dear, you actually mean?

MAY: That's right, and why should *I* do it (*lights another cigarette*), I'm not your slave.

GODBOY (*standing before the cupboard*): Dear?

MAY: What now?

GODBOY: Couldn't this trifling chore be left until later, dear?

MAY: No.

GODBOY: There's a question of fetching something in for Doris and Eric.

MAY: It's fetched, don't you worry.

    (*There's a pause.* MAY *claps her hands again.* MR GODBOY *steps inside the cupboard.*)

MAY: I'm leaving you.

GODBOY (*puts his head out*): Pardon dear?

    (MAY *claps her hands.* MR. GODBOY *goes back in.*)

    (*Shouting.*) Are you still in love with me, dear?

MAY (*laughs*): What?

    (MR. GODBOY *steps fluently out of the cupboard, shuts the door, hurries over to* MAY.)

GODBOY: I've been meaning to inquire for some time, May? (*Sits down beside her.*) It's particularly important for me to know the answer; I'd like to think there's been happiness for you this last two years.

MAY: That's what you like to think, is it?

GODBOY (*folds his hands into his lap*): You've got such an amusing wit, dear. (*Laughing.*) Oh dear.

MAY: I have, have I? (*Little pause.*) What you think you're doing then?

GODBOY (*smiling*): Pardon, dear?

MAY: Get back into that cupboard. I'm not going near it and don't you think I am.

GODBOY (*sits*): The truth is, dear. . . .

    (MAY *claps her hands.* MR. GODBOY *leaps to his feet, hurries over to the cupboard, steps inside. There is a pause.*)

MAY (*half singing*): Oh, I'm leaving you, leaving you, leaving you.

GODBOY: Pardon, dear? (*Head appearing around the cupboard door.*)

MAY: I said, if you was the same kettle of fish as my Number One, you wouldn't have no wound, and if you had, it wouldn't stop you.

GODBOY (*steps out of the cupboard*): Specialists have done their best for me, dear, and still I defeat them all.

MAY: If you was like Number One, you'd learn to handle me. (*Little pause.*) Once he give me a tanning, and I loved him the more for it.

GODBOY (*after a long pause*): I have my own way of doing things, dear. Violence to a living creature is not in my nature.

MAY: What you up to, in and out of there like a rabbit from a top hat. Come on (*claps her hands*) Perkins, come on. (MR. GODBOY *wheels around, goes back into the cupboard. Steps out again almost at once.*)

GODBOY: The truth of the matter is, dear, I'm not feeling exactly on top of myself.

MAY: Oh yes, it's about time for that, isn't it? And something else I've been thinking, if that wound's down there, why does it hurt you up there?

GODBOY: That's what defeats the specialists, dear. (*Clasping his head, comes over, sits down.*) All they know is, if they solve the one they solve the other.

MAY (*gets up, trudges over to the cupboard*): I knew I'd have to do it myself.

GODBOY: No, don't do it, dear, we can do it together after Eric and Doris have left. I'd enjoy that. Just the two of us.

MAY: By then it'll be just the one of us. (*Looks at him.*) I want everything to my hand. (*Nods.*) Besides, knowing Eric he'll forget to come, if there's something at the pictures he wants to see.
(*She goes into the cupboard.* MR. GODBOY *comes over, stands in indecision, looking yearningly in at her.*)

GODBOY: You say he's gone to the pictures.
(*He half reaches for the padlock, takes his hand out, empty.* MAY *comes out with an armful of clothes, drops them on the floor.*)

MAY: That's where he'll be, if I know Eric, he'd be at the pictures if Doris was dying and the world was changing to mud.

19

*(Goes in, comes out with more clothes, drops them down as* MR. GODBOY *comes closer.)*

You must be mad, filling this up with my things, then turning on your wound to get off it. *(Goes in again.)* Oh yes, and it's only the thought of seeing him. . . .

*(*MR. GODBOY, *sidling to the alcove, plunges his hand in behind the curtain.)*

GODBOY? Yes, he forgot last time, didn't he, dear?

*(He slams the cupboard door shut, simultaneously there is a knock on the hall door, right, and* MR. GODBOY *opens the cupboard door again. The shutting. The knocking. The opening. All should come at almost exactly the same instant.* MR. GODBOY *stands holding the cupboard door open, having let go of the pipe. He is smiling courteously.* MAY *comes out, looks at him, steps very close, points a finger into his face.)*

MAY : Now what are you. . . ?

*(The knock comes again. She turns to the hall door, goes towards it.* MR. GODBOY *bends down, picks up armfuls of her clothes puts them back into the cupboard, shuts the cupboard door, as* MAY *opens the hall door.)*

I knew you wouldn't forget your May.

*(She stands aside, to let first* ERIC, *then* DORIS *pass. Smiles at* ERIC. ERIC *is about twenty-five, thin-faced and pale. Black hair slicked back.* DORIS *is about twenty, taller than* ERIC, *her lips are bright red, her finger-nails scarlet. She is wearing a new-look cotton dress, nylon stockings with seams, and stocky, high-heeled shoes. She walks gingerly, with a slight suggestion of a limp. She is holding a handbag pressed close to her stomach.)*

ERIC : Hello May. *(He is wearing a rain-coat and scarf. He walks across the room with one shoulder slightly hunched.)*

DORIS : Hello May.

*(She is watched closely by* MR. GODBOY, *who is standing now to one side, his hands over his crotch.)*

MAY : You're a relief for sore eyes, if you hadn't come I'd have killed you.

GODBOY *(following* DORIS, *who has sat down on the sofa)* : This is a pleasure, Doris *(in a low voice).*

20

(ERIC *sits down in one of the utility chairs, adopting a slouched, tough-looking posture.* MAY *comes to stand beside him, puts a hand on his shoulder.*)

MAY: See anything different in here?

ERIC: What? (*Stares around the room, shakes his head.*) No.

MAY (*bending her face close to his*): Go on, something extra.

(ERIC *stares at* MR. GODBOY, *who is standing between the arm-chair and the sofa.*)

ERIC: Him.

(*There is a pause.*)

I mean, last time he wasn't here, when we come down. (*As* MAY *laughs.*)

DORIS: Yes, there's a——

MAY: Don't spoil it, Doris, let him guess. (*Sharply.*)

ERIC (*shakes his head*): What?

(MAY *puts her hands around his neck, pretending to throttle him. He hunches up, makes cinematic gagging sounds.*)

MAY (*jerks him upright*): Come on then.

ERIC: What?

(MAY *points* ERIC's *face to the cupboard, pretends to throttle him further.*)

MAY: Ooo you! What's that then?

(*Little pause, as* DORIS *and* MR. GODBOY *watch.*)

ERIC: Oh. (*Little pause.*) A shed.

(MAY *screams with laughter, wags* ERIC's *head with her hands, as* MR. GODBOY *sits down beside* DORIS. *Folds his hands into his lap, looks at her, looks at* MAY *and* ERIC.)

MAY: It's a cupboard we got for you, you midge, what do you think of it?

ERIC (*after a pause*): It's big.

GODBOY: It was the most capacious obtainable.

(DORIS *nods.* ERIC *looks at the cupboard, puzzled.*)

MAY: Is that what you could do with?

ERIC: What for?

MAY: For locking Doris up in when she's naughty.

(*She laughs, sits down in the chair opposite* ERIC, *then pulls it close to him.* MR GODBOY *says something to* DORIS *in a low voice.*)

ERIC: What?

GODBOY: I was merely saying to Doris that I'd be able to deal with her tomorrow, if things go as planned.

ERIC: Oh.

(ERIC *looks at* DORIS, *who looks down into her lap.*)

MAY (*to* ERIC): She's lucky, he hasn't touched a foot in six months, except his own, but he'll make an exception out of Doris, and if *you've* got anything coming up, I'll handle it. (*Slaps his knee, laughs.*)

ERIC: Oh, I'm all right, aren't I, Doris?

MAY: That's just the way of it, it's the poor ladies that suffer, it's a good job we don't get corns on our heels. (*To* DORIS.)

DORIS: On my heels?

MAY: On your heels. (*Nods solemnly, then bursts out laughing.*)

ERIC (*joins in*): You can't get corns on your heels.

GODBOY (*to* DORIS): It's a fact that corns can cause as much distress to the whole system as ulcers, which is why I've made arrangements to attend to you properly, Doris.

DORIS: Well (*little pause, looks at* ERIC), I get a bit nervous at being tampered with, see?

ERIC: She's always been like that. Won't go near a doctor.

DORIS: Last time I went he—he—hurt me somewhere.

MAY: Where?

DORIS: Somewhere, that's all.

GODBOY: There's no cause for concern, Doris, I can assure you of that.

MAY (*leans over, slaps* ERIC'S *knee*): You been doing any more your night-walks, then?

ERIC: What? (*To* MAY, *then to* MR. GODBOY.) Can you do for her, then?

GODBOY: Indeed. (*Nods at* DORIS.) I'll do for you, Doris.

DORIS: What will you do then?

GODBOY: There'll be a preliminary examination, Doris, to ascertain the extent of its growth, how deep in the imbedment goes, which will be followed by some probing.

DORIS: Probing? Oh.

MAY (*nodding her head at* ERIC): Here Eric, I heard you come in the other night, it was morning, almost.

ERIC: Oh. (*Nods. Then to* MR. GODBOY.) She won't like too much probing, she's dead against being tampered with.

GODBOY: Probably a mere lotion will do the trick, or I could administer a little whiff, Doris.

MAY (*bends forward to tap* ERIC *on the knee*): What you do out there at night?

ERIC (*looks at her*): Nothing. (*To* DORIS.) That sounds all right, Dorrie.

DORIS: That's all I'm having.

ERIC: Yes, that's her lot.

DORIS: A little whiff of what?

(MAY *wags her head irritably*.)

GODBOY (*after a pause*): That will depend on what other symptoms it's been giving you, Doris, otherwise than its throbbing and its seize.

MAY: That's enough, isn't it.

ERIC: What?

GODBOY (*to* DORIS): Any other inconvenience above the pain?

DORIS (*shakes her head*): Whiff of what, what'll you——

MAY (*simultaneous with* DORIS *and to* MR. GODBOY): Isn't that enough?

GODBOY: In which case the lotion applied on sterile pads, or a little whiff.

DORIS: Well, whiff of what?

MAY (*to* DORIS): Why don't you show it to him now? Go on.

(*There is a pause.* DORIS *looks down at her handbag, which she is clutching to her stomach*.)

MAY: Go on, give us a look.

ERIC (*to* MAY): Here, she don't want to do that.

GODBOY: I appreciate that, Doris.

MAY: Oooo. (*Slaps* ERIC *on the knee*.) Aren't they the bashful two.

ERIC: She's like that. She don't like showing herself off.

MAY: It's only a corn we want to see. Go on, slip off your stockings, dear.

GODBOY (*to* MAY): A chiropodist isn't permitted to take public liberties with his customer's feet, dear.

MAY: A chopidist isn't pitted to show his customer's feet, dear.

23

(*Imitating contemptuously.*) Oooh dear. Don't worry, chopidist, nobody wants to see people's feet at a party, it's music we want. Put a record on, Eric.

ERIC: What? Oh. Righto. (*Gets up, walks over to the gramophone, picks up a record, scans the cover closely and uncomprehendingly, puts it down, picks up another.*)

MAY (*to* DORIS): You going to have a fling with the chopidist?

DORIS (*who is staring straight ahead*): I can't.

MAY: Course you can, what do you mean, can't?

DORIS (*voice quavering*) I can't dance with that foot.

MAY: Dance with the other one, then. (*Laughs.*) Or borrow one from the chopidist.

GODBOY (*to* ERIC, *who has been watching him*): Eric, old boy, if you'll excuse my mentioning it, that one's not for dancing to.

ERIC (*who has been about to put the needle on*): What?

MAY (*to* MR. GODBOY): What do you know about what's for dancing to? Eric and me can dance to anything. (*Gets up, goes to the centre of the room, makes dancing movements.*) Put it on, Eric.

ERIC: Oh. Righto. (*Looks at* MR. GODBOY, *looks at* MAY, *puts the record on.*) We'll just have a quick one, Dorrie.
(*The record begins. It is one of Churchill's war speeches. *ERIC* stands by the gramophone, bewildered. *DORIS* looks down at her handbag, *MAY* stands still. *MR. GODBOY* gets up, walks right across, takes the record off, puts it back in its cover, goes back, sits down.*)
Who was that then?

GODBOY (*after a pause*): That was Winnie, old boy.
(MAY *goes to the record pile.* ERIC *joins her, they begin to sort through the records.*)
(*To* DORIS.) Five years ago there wasn't a man in this country wouldn't have laid down his life for Winnie, and glad to do it.
(MAY *whispers something to* ERIC, *laughs.*)
Of course the war wouldn't mean much to Eric, as he was safe out of it, I'm glad to say for his sake.

ERIC (*turning*): What?

GODBOY: I was merely wondering, Eric, where were you
    precisely when the V.2's commenced dropping?
ERIC: Me?
GODBOY: In 1944 to be frank, old boy. Where were you precisely?
ERIC (*thinks, looks at* DORIS): I was in Wales, wasn't I Dorrie, in
    that home?
GODBOY: Now refresh my memory, old boy, were there V.2s
    dropping in Wales?
ERIC: V. what? (*Little pause.*) Here, I never had nothing like
    that. (*Indignantly.*)
MAY (*puts a record on the gramophone*): What you going on at
    him for—you'd have ridden on a V.2 if they'd let you
    wear your special constable uniform. This one (*as the
    music starts*) was too nice and young to get messed up in
    that.
    (*She holds out her arms, they start to dance,* ERIC *glancing
    apprehensively at* DORIS.)
    (MAY *leads* ERIC *further into a corner of the room, dancing
    amorously,* DORIS *and* MR GODBOY *watching.*)
GODBOY: Indeed Eric was too young for combat, and I don't
    hold it against him, Doris.
    (DORIS *goes on watching the dancing, tense.*)
    But there was—were some youths on the other side who
    weren't too young. Mere children of nine were issued with
    pitchforks and ordered to stand and resist. Those were the
    sort of people Winnie had to stamp out (*stamps his foot*) to
    make the country safe for the likes of Eric, who is a very
    pleasant boy, as I'm the first to admit. They didn't teach
    him to read in Wales then?
    (*Little pause.* DORIS *shakes her head.*)
    So frankly, between you and me, Doris, as May and Eric
    wouldn't understand as they naturally like to enjoy them-
    selves, that's why I'm against having that record put on for
    joking at. Those were terrible days. (*Little pause.*) And that
    record brings back happy memories of them. How's your
    toe now?
    (DORIS *shrugs.*)
    I hadn't forgotten about it, Doris, there was something I

had to get out of the way first, which I'm dealing with now. (*Looks at* MAY.)

(*The music stops.* MAY *does a grotesque curtsey.* ERIC *laughs, looks towards* DORIS, *sees her face, stops laughing.* MAY *looks at* DORIS *and* MR. GODBOY, *keeps a hold on* ERIC'*s arm.*)

MAY: What's he off on now, the double Dublin tenant and wife gasser?

ERIC: What?

MAY: His head is filled with murder, that's all he thinks about, isn't it, chopidist? That and Inspector Manly Mannerly Irish Hawkins.

GODBOY: Indeed, dear, I keep in touch, merely.

MAY (*to* ERIC): Come on, let's get our hands on something I've got special in the kitchen.

(*Leads him towards the kitchen. He looks at* DORIS, *who glares at him.*)

(DORIS *and* MR. GODBOY *sit stiffly on the sofa, staring straight ahead. There are noises from the kitchen, a crashing sound, a scream of* MAY'*s laughter. A pause. Then* MR. GODBOY *gets up, goes to the gramophone. As he does so,* ERIC *comes in, his coat and scarf over his arm, looks at* DORIS, *who turns away from him, plods across the room to the cupboard, opens it.*)

GODBOY (*with his back to* ERIC *and* DORIS): My interest in murder is connected to my interest in police work, Doris, needless to say, which goes back a long way. My years as Special Constable during the war naturally heightened my interest. That's all there is to it, in spite of May's hints, I hope you won't. . . .

(MR. GODBOY *turns, as* ERIC, *having shut the door of the cupboard, walks back across the room to the kitchen door. Watches him.* ERIC *looks at* DORIS, *whose face is still averted, stands at the kitchen door.*)

ERIC: Well, I'll just. . . .

(*He shrugs, nods, goes into the kitchen, leaves door open.* DORIS *sits staring ahead.* MR. GODBOY *looks towards the kitchen door, from which comes a scream of* MAY'*s laughter: goes towards it to shut it when it slams noisily from inside.*

*He stops. Goes back to the sofa, sits down. There is a pause).*

GODBOY: May has a funny sense of humour, she makes me
chuckle out loud sometimes. (*Little pause.*) You can't
understand the workings of murder until you understand
the workings of the police. The two things are connected.
(*Little pause.*) Do you follow me there, Doris?
(*Throughout the following conversation there are noises from
the kitchen, mainly of* MAY's *laughter, but gradually with*
ERIC's *joining in.*)

DORIS (*shrugs*): I don't like the police?

GODBOY (*swings his head around, looks at her*): Indeed? I'm
sorry to hear you say that, Doris, very sorry. Have you any
grounds?

DORIS (*shrugs. After a long pause, looks down at her handbag*):
They searched me once. In front of—people.

GODBOY (*after a pause*): Well, Doris, justice has not only got to
be done, it's got to be seen to be done. That's what makes
our country great. (*Pause.*) I'm sure you'll admit they did
a good job of it.
(*Long pause, as* DORIS *continues to stare down.*)
Pardon a little ignorance, unfortunately searching wasn't
one of my duties, how far exactly did they authorize
themselves to go?

DORIS (*whispering*): Everything. They took off me everything.

GODBOY: Indeed? (*Long pause.*) That would include, pardon my
asking, to get the details straight in my head (*puts a hand
to his head*), stockings, under-garments such as for instance
cami-knicks and bra, naturally? (*Little pause.*) Am I right
in my guess?

DORIS: Me everything.

GODBOY: Yes, they've got to be thorough. (*Little pause.*) It was
male officers took part in this.

DORIS: They was peeking. One of them was.

GODBOY: Superintending the legality, Doris, merely, that's all.
Can you remember who it was precisely? Did you see his
face?

DORIS: I don't know, I kept me eyes down.

GODBOY (*after a pause*): Indeed. (*Little pause.*) As a matter of

27

interest, Doris, and strictly privately, May's likely to go off on a little trip.

(*Sudden scream of laughter from* MAY.)

DORIS: Oh? She never said.

GODBOY: No, I intend it to come as a complete and utter surprise to her. She won't know about it until she's on her way, virtually.

(*Another scream of laughter.*)

She's got it coming to her, she deserves a long rest.

DORIS: When's she going then?

(*Little pause.*)

GODBOY: I've got it planned so that with luck she'll be gone by tomorrow.

(*Waits through another scream.*)

I think I can promise you that.

DORIS: That'll be nice.

GODBOY (*turns his head, looks at her*): I'm glad you've said that, Doris.

(*The kitchen door opens, and* ERIC *puts his head around it. He is grinning.*)

ERIC: Who's for stout, then?

(*Little pause.*)

GODBOY: No thank you, Eric.

(ERIC *looks straight at* DORIS. *She stares ahead.*)

ERIC: Dorrie?

(*She continues to stare ahead.*)

Dorrie? (ERIC *looks at her a moment longer, withdraws, closes the door.*)

DORIS: Is she going a long way away?

GODBOY: Purley, probably. (*Little pause.*) I only mention it now merely so you won't wonder at her abrupt disappearance tomorrow.

(*The door opens again.* ERIC, *grinning, puts his head in.*)

ERIC: Who's for a drop of something else, then?

(MR. GODBOY *looks at him,* DORIS *stares straight ahead.*)

She's got a bottle of gin in there.

GODBOY: No thank you, Eric.

ERIC: Dorrie?

*(She continues to stare ahead.)*

What?

*(Withdraws his head, shuts the door. There is a burst of laughter from* MAY.*)*

GODBOY *(after a pause)*: How do you feel about that surprise news, Doris?

DORIS *(after another scream)*: It'll be quiet without her.

GODBOY: Indeed. *(Nods.)* That's one thing I'm expecting. *(Little pause.)* It would be best if I was to arrange our appointment now. *(Takes the padlock out of his pocket, puts it back hurriedly, takes out a diary.)* As you now realize I shall be free as of tomorrow on. I'll be ready to get down to it before it's too late. *(There is a silence.)* I'm referring to your toe, Doris. What do you say to tomorrow tea-time? *(*MR. GODBOY *looks at* DORIS, *who shrugs nervously, looks down.)*

Righto, tomorrow tea-time?

DORIS: What is, I mean, this whiff you was—whiff of something. . . .

*(The door opens.* ERIC *comes in. He is slightly drunk.)*

ERIC: Comfy? *(Long pause.)* That May. *(Laughs.)*

DORIS *(looks at him vindictively)*: May's going away tomorrow.

*(*MR. GODBOY *looks at her.)*

ERIC: She hasn't said nothing.

GODBOY: Only you're to keep it quiet, old boy, it's a surprise to May, don't let anything drop.

*(*ERIC *thinks. Laughs.)*

Why do you laugh, old boy?

ERIC: Well, she keeps saying she's got a surprise laid up for you.

GODBOY: Indeed? What type of surprise precisely, Eric?

ERIC: She won't tell, she keeps tapping her nose and laughing over it, but I got a part in it.

GODBOY: Indeed, Eric, what's that?

ERIC: You got to wait. *(Holds up his hand.)* Eh, Dorrie?

*(She stares ahead. There is a silence, then the sound of a lavatory flushing off, right, and the door, right, opens.* MAY *enters the room, one arm raised, she looks at* ERIC, *they lower their arms simultaneously and begin to sing.)*

29

MAY \ (*as* MAY *advances on* MR. GODBOY): Now is the hour.
ERIC: / When I must say good-bye.

> (*They sing the song through,* MR. GODBOY *and* DORIS *sitting staring straight ahead, until the last few lines, when* MR. GODBOY *begins to sing. He sings the last line by himself as* MAY *throws herself laughing into* ERIC'S *arms and lights dim.*)

### Scene 2

*Lights up. Half an hour later.* DORIS *and* MR. GODBOY *still sitting on the sofa, staring directly ahead. There is a sound of a door slamming, the kitchen-hall door, left.* MAY *comes in through the kitchen door, left. She is carrying a glass. She sits down on one of the utility chairs, left, drinks from her glass.* MR. GODBOY *and* DORIS *watch her.*

DORIS (*after a pause, voice quavering*): Where's Eric then?
MAY (*sipping from her glass*): Gone, dear.

> (*There is a little silence.*)

DORIS: Where?
MAY: Don't know. (*Little pause.*) Last I saw he was lurching down the hall. (*Looks at her sharply.*) Where's he go most nights, I hear him coming in all hours.
DORIS (*after a pause*): For walks. (*Pause.*) He said he's stop. He said he wouldn't any more.
GODBOY: Doubtless he'll come straight in up to the flat, Doris.
MAY: Doubtless. (*Little pause. Looks at* DORIS): What for?
> (*Little pause.*) Oh, drink puts Eric in a talking mood, we got the same problems, Eric and me. (*Shakes his head.*) But I'm getting over mine.
GODBOY: Pardon, dear.
MAY: She knows what I mean. (*Stares at* DORIS.)

> (DORIS, *after a pause, gets up, stands for a moment with her handbag, half opened, clasped to her stomach, then walks limping to the door, right.*)
> (*Silkily.*) Good-bye, dear.

30

(MR. GODBOY *gets up, follows* DORIS, *holds the door open
for her.*)

GODBOY: Good night, Doris.

DORIS: He said he wouldn't go out nights any more.

GODBOY: Don't you worry about him, Doris, he'll be back in no
time. (*Little pause.*) And see you as arranged (*slapping his
pocket*), tea-time.

(DORIS *goes out.* MR. GODBOY *puts his head into the hall,
watches for a second, then shuts the door, comes back.*
MAY *drinks from her glass and watches him.*)

MAY: Coming tomorrow is she?

GODBOY: Pardon dear? Oh, yes, tomorrow seemed best.

MAY: Well, you'll have a free hand tomorrow.

(MR. GODBOY *looks at her.*)

Not that a free hand with her's worth a eunuch's while.

GODBOY: Pardon dear?

(MAY *looks at him, shrugs, drinks.*)

(*After a pause.*) Well dear, that was a pleasant evening, I
must say.

MAY: Must you? Why?

(MR. GODBOY *stares at her.*)

Why must you say it?

GODBOY: I thought you must be enjoying yourself. (*Long pause.*)
Who's for bed, dear?

MAY: Pardon, dear? (*Mimicking.*)

(MR. GODBOY *laughs. There is a pause. He goes to the
cupboard, swerves on to the guppies.* MAY *sits watching him.
He turns, looks, nods, smiles.*)

GODBOY: Well dear, (*stretches*) well (*yawns*) I need my bed, I
must—(*stops himself*).

MAY: What for?

GODBOY: Why, for a good night's sleep, dear.

MAY: That what you think I need?

GODBOY: Par——

MAY (*simultaneously*): Pardon dear? A good night's sleep which
is you curled up and clinging to the edge of your side like
a winkle. A good night's sleep, which is me blinking into
the darkness and thinking about what I had with Number

31

One and how it won't never come no more. (*Little pause.*)
Why do you wear two pair of pyjamas?

GODBOY: Merely, dear because I'm susceptible to cold, just as
you prefer your hottie, why do you ask?

MAY: My hottie's got more bed-life in it than you have. (*Pause.*)
You know what I'm trying to say to you?

GODBOY: No dear.

MAY: Can't you even guess?

GODBOY (*after a little pause*): No dear.

MAY: More fool you, then. (*Slowly, significantly.*)
(*She gets up, goes to the kitchen, leaves the door open.* MR
GODBOY *looks at the cupboard, then towards the kitchen door.
Goes on tiptoe to the kitchen door, shuts it. Then hurries to
the cupboard.*)
(*Flinging open the kitchen door.*) Leave it open.
(MR. GODBOY *stops, turns around.*)
Leave it open. I've had enough of you closing things up on
me, now I'm after space.
(*She goes to the door, left, opens it, goes into the bedroom.*
MR. GODBOY *stares after her, then goes quietly to the cup-
board, opens it. Goes to the alcove, checks the cylinder, then
turns around, goes to the guppies.*)

GODBOY: Don't forget your night-things in the cupboard, dear.
I've left the door open for you to make your selection from.
(MAY *appears at the bedroom door, holding a suitcase open.
She stares at him. He stays bent away from her, gestures
with his hands backwards.*)
I was merely reminding you of your nighties.

MAY: Yes, I'll be needing those. (*Significantly.*)
(*She walks across to the cupboard, steps in.* MR. GODBOY
*whirls round, suddenly remembers padlock, snatches it out,
turns the key to open it, opens it, drops the key, picks the
key up, makes a go at putting it back, then frantically puts it
in his mouth, steals across, puts the padlock open and ready
in the door-jamb hook, then key still in his mouth, whips to
the alcove, grabs the tubing, reaches for the door with his
left hand, as* MAY *steps out with the clothes.* MR. GODBOY
*slams the door, whirls around.* MAY *turns as he holds the*

*tubing behind him, walks up to him, puts her face close to his.*)

(*Shouts.*) Stop slamming, I said.

(*She gives him a push with her arms.* MR. GODBOY *steps back, swallows the key, as* MAY *turns away.*)

Open it up again.

MR. GODBOY *stands watching, swallowing and coughing slightly as* MAY *disappears into the bedroom, then gagging a little, opens the cupboard door, stands with the pipe held down, waiting.*

(*Calling.*) You wouldn't notice if the house was collapsing around your eyes.

GODBOY: True, dear, very true.

(*He swallows experimentally.* MAY *reappears, begins to hum "Now is the hour. . . ."*

MAY (*stares at him*): What you doing then?

GODBOY (*holding the pipe behind him*): Thinking merely, dear.

MAY: About murder merely dear?

(GODBOY *laughs.*)

Or about how much you'd miss me merely dear?

GODBOY (*laughs again. Wags his head*): Oh May! (*Coughs again.*)

(MAY *comes towards him, stands in front of him.*)

MAY: Oooh you. (*Shakes her head.*) Ape!

(*Turns, plods back towards the door, left, stops, turns, goes back to the cupboard.* MR. GODBOY *watches tensely. She stands in front of it, half enters it.* MR. GODBOY *moves forward.* MAY *turns.*)

No. (*Holds up a hand.*) No, not now you don't, no help from you thank you. Go nurse your wound. (*Significantly.*) You're too *late.*

(MR. GODBOY *stops, takes a pace back.* MAY *enters the cupboard.* MR. GODBOY *leaps forward. There is a knock on the door, right. He stops, stares towards it.*)

(*Now bending down, her buttocks sticking out of the cupboard.*) Answer it, then.

(MR. GODBOY *hesitates, then thrusts the pipe back into the alcove, goes towards the door, opens it a fraction.*)

GODBOY: Oh. (*Little pause.*) Hello.

(MAY *is now down on all fours, buttocks sticking out of the cupboard.*)

DORIS: (*Voice off.*)

(MR. GODBOY *stares in agony at the cupboard, into which* MAY *has vanished. Holds the door open.* DORIS *walks gingerly a few steps into the room.*)

GODBOY (*stares at* DORIS): I should tell you in all fairness we was—were just preparing ourselves for beddy-byes. (*Laughs.*) Doris.

DORIS (*frightened*): Eric's not there!

GODBOY: Indeed!

(*He glances towards the cupboard.* MAY'*s buttocks reappear, slowly.* DORIS *watches.*)

Well, I can assure he's not with May or me, I'm afraid to say. (*Holds the door open wide.*) Have you glanced in your toilet?

DORIS (*shakes her head*): He's not there.

GODBOY: In which case I gladly give you permission to knock on our toilet.

DORIS: He's not there.

(MR. GODBOY *watches* MAY *back out of the cupboard, an armful of clothes held to her waist. She looks at* DORIS, *shakes her head contemptuously, then goes across to the room left.*)

GODBOY: Indeed? Not in the toilets you say. You do surprise me, but it merely means he must be somewhere else.

(*He watches* MAY *come out of the room, go into the cupboard again.*)

DORIS: He said he wouldn't any more, he said, he does funny things when he's had too much.

(*She stares at* MAY'*s back accusingly.* MR. GODBOY'*s head moves in anguish between* DORIS *and the cupboard.*)

GODBOY: Not to worry, Doris, my advice to you is to phone the hospitals from the corner call-box.

DORIS: Hospitals!

GODBOY (*as* MAY *comes out again*): They have the authority to put you in touch with the latest accident cases and mortuary victims. So not to worry—May dear!

34

DORIS: No he doesn't get hurt, he goes round and round, he says his head does.

GODBOY: Now Doris, that covers hospitals, mortuaries, toilets, which is all I can think of at the moment (*desperately as* MAY *comes back*), so pop upstairs and get a good night's rest. (*He steps in front of the cupboard with his arms out.*) May dear, did you hear that? Eric has mysteriously vanished!

(MAY *stops, looks at him, looks at* DORIS, *shakes her head contemptuously.*)

MAY: What a pair, oooh you lovely things, he's gone to clear his head, like I told you. (*Stares at* DORIS.) And if he *had* gone for a bit of something else, I wouldn't blame him.

(MR. GODBOY *resolutely stands before the cupboard as* MAY *tries to pass.*)

GODBOY: But we have reason to believe that the situation could develop into something more seriously tragic, dear. Doris is thinking in terms of fatal accidents.

MAY (*after a moment, looking from one to the other*): I'll tell you something, the same what I've been telling him.

(*She nods to* MR. GODBOY, *who as* MAY *goes to stand close to* DORIS, *is attempting to shut the cupboard door behind his back against a piece of hanging-out cloth.*)

Because this is the last chance I'll get as things down here have come to a head at last, and that's if you made your Eric welcome, he'd be up there, inside, and you know who I mean, who a man ought to be inside of. You don't give him what he needs, Doris Hoyden, and he'll do what I'm doing to him, who doesn't give me the same.

(*She nods at* MR. GODBOY, *who has now turned around and wrestling with the cupboard door face on.*)

GODBOY: Indeed dear, there's no doubt about that.

MAY: Or you'll end up like him, hanging about the police station and chasing after a Inspector Hawkins as if he'd do his work for him.

GODBOY (*shuts the cupboard at last, turns around, stands against the door grinning*): Exactly what I say to you, Doris, let the police handle it.

(*There is the squeal of tyres outside. Pause. They listen.*)

DORIS: Oh no, no, I'm not going near them.

MAY: Ooooh what a pair! (*Turns, goes to the door, stops, looks back, shakes her head, goes into the room, left.*)

GODBOY: Now Doris dear, as May says, not to worry, not to worry. Also as May says, there's the police outside near at hand, you could go and bother them, I merely mean (*goes to the hall door, rights, opens it*) this tramping about isn't doing our corn any good, and the best thing for you all said and done is to aim for some shut-eye. (*He holds the door open, gestures usheringly out of the door, stops, cocks his head.*) And who's that coming in now if I'm not mistaken.

(*He steps out into the hall, DORIS behind him.*)

(*HAWKINS, as yet unseen, says something inaudible. MR. GODBOY backs into the room, forcing DORIS back behind him.*) That is my name, yes.

HAWKINS: (*Says something else.*)

(*MR. GODBOY stands at the door as DORIS peers over his shoulder, stares in alarm, then hurries away, goes to sit down in a corner of the sofa, her face turned away.*)

GODBOY: Indeed, sir, indeed.

(*He stands aside to let HAWKINS in. His face wears an expression of bemused reverence. HAWKINS steps in, steps out again. His voice audible in a shout.*)

HAWKINS: All right boys, wait out in the car there and keep the engine humming, boys. (*He enters. He is wearing a smart suit, a carnation in his button-hole. And is carrying a trilby. He is tall, broad-shouldered, flush-faced, tough-looking, forty-five. He comes past MR. GODBOY into the centre of the room, looks at DORIS, who is facing away, nods.*) Evening ma'am.

(*DORIS nods, mumbles, without looking at him. MR. GODBOY stands staring at HAWKINS' back in a kind of rapture. Then holds out his hand, advances around him at the precise moment that HAWKINS revolves, so that again MR. GODBOY's hand is held out to HAWKINS' back. Drops his hand, clears his throat as HAWKINS turns again. They face each other.*)

36

GODBOY: Pardon me, sir, but it is Inspector Hawkins sir, isn't it? This is an honour, sir. (*Little pause.*) Indeed.

HAWKINS: Thank you, Mr. Godboy, Duty Officer Larkin said I'd be known on the premises if I took the liberty of dropping in out of the night. (*Looks at* DORIS.)

GODBOY (*nodding*): We was colleagues during the war years, sir, in a manner of speaking, and recently since you've been back I've exchanged nods at you down at the station, sir, although doubtless you've been too much on the job to pay them much attention.

(*As he holds out his hand again tentatively,* HAWKINS *goes smoothly over to* DORIS, *at whom he has been smiling.*)

HAWKINS: And is it Mrs. Godboy then?

(DORIS *shakes her head, looks away.*)

GODBOY (*coming over*): No, Mrs. Godboy is busy in the bed-room, her work there is never done, as they say (*picks up quickly a few of the clothes* MAY *has dropped*), although I'm particularly anxious for her to meet you. (*Straightens.*) This young lady's from the upstairs premises, she's lost her husband for the moment. (*Laughs.*) May, dear! May! (*Goes over, knocks on the door.*) May! (*Opens the door, shoves the clothes in while calling out.*) There's someone here I'm anxious for you to meet.

(HAWKINS *has been standing close to* DORIS, *who sits tight, staring ahead.*)

HAWKINS: Lost your husband, have you, if he's missing too long, you call on us then.

GODBOY: May, dear, there's Inspector Hawkins himself in the parlour.

HAWKINS (*winks, nods at* DORIS): The husbands we can't return, we replace. (*Laughs.*)

DORIS (*in a whisper*): Thank you.

(MAY *appears at the door,* MR. GODBOY *in front of her. She has a mountain of clothes in her arms.* MR. GODBOY *steps around her, puts an arm around her waist, clears his throat to attract* HAWKINS' *attention.* MAY *stares at* HAWKINS *cynically.*)

HAWKINS (*turns*): I was just saying to the young lady, there's a pick of the boys at the station.

GODBOY (*laughs*): I've been hoping that you two was—would come face to face before too late, too long, I merely—the idea of it means a lot to me, this is my wife, Inspector Hawkins, May Godboy.

HAWKINS (*nods, smiles, revolves his trilby in his hands*): It's a great pleasure m'am.

(MAY *drops a few clothes from the top of the pile which* MR. GODBOY *tries to catch, then bends down to pick up.*)

MAY: It's the dream of his life, to show you off at me.

GODBOY (*straightening, puts the clothes back on the pile*): Pardon dear? (*As a few more clothes drop from the bottom of the pile, laughs, bends down again.*)

MAY: And he only just pulled it off, a day later you'd have missed me.

HAWKINS: Now I call that flattering. (*Little pause.*) You're taking a trip, are you?

GODBOY (*now fishing between* MAY's *legs for an article of under-clothing*): Pardon, sir? A trip (*laughs*), no, not that she knows of, eh, May dear, oops, pardon, dear.

MAY: I might be. (*Nods.*)

HAWKINS (*laughs*): Ah, the ladies need little trips as much as the ladies' husbands.

(*He turns, does a nod-wink at* DORIS, *who is still staring desperately ahead.*)

GODBOY: Pardon? (*Straightens, looks smiling from one to the other.*)

MAY: Have you come to arrest him, he spends all his time down at that station of yours he'd be better in the nog behind it.

GODBOY (*laughs, takes all the clothes out of* MAY's *arms*): Not even Inspector Hawkins can arrest me *before* I commit my offence, May dear. (*He goes into the bedroom.*)

HAWKINS: No, the truth is, m'am, that cruising around in the neighbourhood, with a spot of waiting ahead of me, I remembered Larkins mentioning Mr. Godboy's name, and thinking to meet some of the people on top of it all (*turns, nods at* DORIS), I thought to myself, why not look in for a

38

minute as the lights from your home were cheering up the
darkness, like an invitation it seemed. (*Turns, nods to*
DORIS *again*.) If I'm not intruding, that is.

MAY: Well, where's this female constable they're all talking
about that's turned up so sudden, don't I get to see her?

HAWKINS (*little pause*): Is it Constable Hedderley you mean?
(*As* MR. GODBOY *comes back out of the room, stands beside*
MAY *again*.)
Well, to tell you a secret (*turns to look at* DORIS), Constable
Hedderley's out on a very special duty just a minute or
two away, so if you hear a strange commotion, as will be
the ringing of police bells, the blowing of police whistles,
the barking of police dogs, it'll be that Constable Hedderley's pulled it off and I'll be on my way in a hurry.

GODBOY: The Merrit Street case!

HAWKINS (*after a pause, looks at* MR. GODBOY): Well, and so it
is. There's the mind of a natural policeman for you.
(MR. GODBOY *swells proudly, looks at* MAY, *who turns her
face from him*.)
I gave orders there was to be no gossip, so I'll be having a
word or two that'll boil Larkins' ears in the morning
(*laughs, nods at* DORIS), but there's no harm in mentioning
it now, as you're under my personal eye (*nods to* DORIS
*again*), the truth is that Constable Hedderley's under a
street lamp and fiddling in the line of duty with suspenders
and stockings and generally behaving temptingly, and all
about Merrit Street the boys are scattered, waiting for the
attacker to start his indecent assault on our provocative
piece of bait, who's also carrying a handbag to tempt him
further.

GODBOY: Masterly, Mannerly, Masterly.
(HAWKINS *looks at him*.)

MAY: Yes that's nice, but what if he gets into this Hedderley
before they get there, or can't stop him once he gets going.
There's some men I knew, one in particular I was married
to once (*looks at* MR. GODBOY), couldn't have been bombed
off a lady he'd get that——
(HAWKINS *laughs, winks-nods to* DORIS.)

GODBOY: Now my dear, all of Inspector Hawkins' finest combined can handle any man going.

HAWKINS: Don't you worry, m'am, Constable Hedderley will toss him off as soon as look at him.

MAY: Oh, will she! (*Lets out a screech of laughter.*)
(HAWKINS *laughs, nods towards* DORIS. MR. GODBOY, *baffled, chuckles.*)

MAY (*after a silence*): Yes, it's not only from him I heard about you, Manly.
(HAWKINS *looks at her. Chuckles.* MAY *chuckles.* HAWKINS *looks towards* DORIS, *who smiles awkwardly, goes on chuckling.*)

HAWKINS: Well no, no, I have to keep myself free to move in any direction. I can be to Hedderley's side in thirty seconds with the car waiting, so don't you disturb yourself on Hedderley's account, ma'am.

GODBOY: That's what they mean by springing a trap, dear.

MAY: Yes, well I got to do some springing myself, out of my own trap.
(*She unwinds* MR. GODBOY'*s arm, which has replaced itself around her waist, goes back into the room, slams the door.* MR. GODBOY *turns, stares after her, then opens the door, puts his head in as* HAWKINS *goes over, stands near to* DORIS, *smiles at her, nods.*)

GODBOY: What about a cup for Inspector Mannerly Hawkins, dear?
(MAY *says something inaudible but clearly abusive.* MR. GODBOY *emerges, embarrassed, looks towards where* HAWKINS *was, then turns to where he is now, standing beside* DORIS.)
As I say, her work is never done. (*Little pause, then significantly*), although it soon will be, if I finish off a little plan of mine.
(*Pause.* HAWKINS *continues to smile at* DORIS, *who sits stiffly, smiling, staring ahead.*)
Would you care for a (*looks about him*) stout, sir?

HAWKINS (*shakes his head*): Oh, no, no, thank you very much, only if there's one available.

GODBOY : Indeed there is. (*He hurries to the kitchen.*)

HAWKINS (*to* DORIS): I hope I haven't been frightening you,
    ma'am, with my talk of the Merrit Street rapist?
    (DORIS *shakes her head.*)
    We come into contact with such terrible things, we forget
    the peace of mind of the innocent. (*Little pause.*) Ah, but
    still the city's a place at night, a violent place, and there's
    not a corner in it you can't hear it's horror come screaming
    for you, if you stand there listening still as a nun. (*Little
    pause.*) Do you know what I mean?
    (DORIS *nods.*)
    (*Looks at her.*) When I was a boy, and yourself a girl, we
    wouldn't have believed it then,
    (DORIS *looks quickly up again, then down.*)
    would we? (*Little pause.*) And now I go about like all the
    nuns that ever were, waiting for the messages or listening
    to the screams, and it's only when I'm talking with someone
    like yourself, ma'am, that I remember there was a time of
    innocence for all of us. (*Little pause.*) And that's the truth.
    (MR. GODBOY *enters, carrying a bottle of stout, and a glass.
    As he pours the stout.*)

GODBOY : This is indeed good news about the Merrit Street case.
    It'll mean another feather in your cap, Man—Inspector,
    rape rates almost as high as murder in some quarters
    (HAWKINS *still looking at* DORIS.)
    although not (*significantly, handing* HAWKINS *the drink*) in
    my own personal opinion, frankly.

HAWKINS (*takes the glass, nods*): My best to you, Mr. Godboy,
    ma'am.
    (*Holding the glass in toast, quickly to* MR. GODBOY, *then a
    fraction longer to* DORIS, *sips, stares about the room, sees the
    guppies.*)

GODBOY (*clears his throat*): In——

HAWKINS (*saunters over to the case*): Goldfish, now?

GODBOY : Um, no sir, in fact known as guppies, sir. Gups
    (*laughs*), we call them.

HAWKINS : And what nimble little fellows they are, darting this
    way and that (*bending over*), I like them, I like them for

41

their speed.

(MR. GODBOY *comes over to the guppie case, stands on the other side, bends over it.*)

GODBOY: Yes, they are quick, very quick. (*Puts a finger in reflectively.*) Inspector there's a question um I'd be interested to hear your personal view on.

(*As* HAWKINS *moves smoothly back to* DORIS, *sits down in one of the utility chairs next to her.*)

Do you think of your top murderer as a basically common or garden chap?

(HAWKINS *whimsically offers his glass to* DORIS, *who shakes her head, looks down into her lap.*)

I merely ask, because there's no doubt that some types of it are on the increase, although I've got no sympathies for the wounded veterans back from the front who lay about harmless old ladies for petty cash.

(*As again* HAWKINS *offers* DORIS *his glass, with an insistent nods and smile.*)

No, I've no time for them, that's a mixture of bad experiences and bad upbringing on the part of soft parents.

(*As* DORIS *is finally forced to take a sip.*)

No, I'm referring to a different specimen altogether, your cool-blooded killer who has the nerve and is prepared to go through with it to the final consequences, as in the case of O'Higgs, the wife and female-tenant gasser, for instance, merely.

(*He looks up, looks around, sees* HAWKINS *sipping from his stout, stares at him. There is a pause.*)

As you may remember, sir, I've had a little time on the force to my credit.

HAWKINS: Oh yes, a special constable wasn't it? (*Sips.*) Not quite a fully-paid up street-beater like myself.

GODBOY: Indeed. Unfortunately I was disqualified from submitting a full application owing to a mixture of age and a wound sustained in an accident. A rough-house that got beyond itself. (*Little pause.*) Children will be children, no blame was officially attached although malice was definitely involved. (*Comes over, sits down beside* HAWKINS *in the other utility chair.*) Pardon me. Of course, a lot if it was checking padlocks in the evening, Mannerly, giving tea to the bombed-outs which between you and me—and is no secret—made nuisances of themselves when in a state of shock and had to be restrained, and added to which there was molest-arrest—taking into custody. (*Shaking his head.*) I merely mean aliens who had no business in the country in the first place and had to be locked up in the interests of the security of the nation.

(*Little pause, as* HAWKINS *sips again, looks towards* DORIS.) But mainly on the whole I was called on to assist in breaking the news in cases of fatal disasters. (*Little pause.*) I sometimes spent six hours a day in breaking tragic news, Inspector Manly, as you can imagine, I tried to do it politely but firmly.

(MAY *comes out of the room, left, walks around to the cupboard, opens it, looks in.* MR. GODBOY *watches, then as* MAY *looks in the second cupboard.*)

HAWKINS: So (*slowly*) you might say you did all our dirtiest work for us?

GODBOY: It was an honour (*watching* MAY) Hawkins, Manly, Inspector Hawkins. (*Laughs.*) Can I help dear?

(*As* MAY *comes back across the room, leaving the cupboard doors open, and entering the room, left.*)

Her work is never——

(*Interrupted by the slamming of the door.*)

Um (*little pause*), indeed, it's because of my time on the force that I'm never likely to be one of those who'd forget our Pierpoint. . . .

HAWKINS: Pierpoint?

GODBOY: Winnie, I merely mean, Inspector. (*Shakes his head, gets up, goes to the cupboard doors, shuts them.*) Pardon me, or runs about like lots of them do nowadays making a mockery out of due procedure in the country especially. . . . (*Comes back, stops, as the door, left, opens,* MAY *stands there for a second then slams the door.*)

Her work is never—(*laughs*) especially when it's an established fact (*sits down*) that it's always properly and

43

ceremoniously carried out with chaplains, doctors and
officials in attendance.

(*Pause, looks at* HAWKINS, *who stares at him.*)

HAWKINS (*after a pause*): Is it hanging you're talking about,
then?

GODBOY: Indeed sir. (*Nods.*) It's my own personal considered
opinion now you bring the subject into the open, frankly,
that a man who is going to end up that way knows about
it long before, from day-dreams and other symptoms, as in
the case of (*little pause, looks at* HAWKINS *hard*) the gasser
O'Higgs, for instance.

HAWKINS (*after a long pause, drains off his glass, stares into it*):
Mr. Godboy—(*slight pause*) Mr. Godboy, would you have
something I could wash this down with, now?

GODBOY: Oh. Well, I'm sorry to say that was the last of the
stout, there's nothing left in the kitchen except some gin
and of course water.

HAWKINS: Now that would be very nice, that's very kind, a
glass of gin and water would do the trick for me nicely,
Mr. Godboy.

GODBOY (*gets up, takes* HAWKINS' *glass*): An honour, Mannerly.
(*Goes out into the kitchen.*)

HAWKINS (*after a pause*): Tell me, ma'am, I think I've forgotten
your name already, or never asked in my rudeness.

DORIS (*in a low voice*): Doris Hoyden.

HAWKINS: Ah. (*Little pause.*) And I've never seen you before,
Doris Hoyden?

(DORIS *shakes her head.*)

It's as if I'd had a peep of you sometime, there are little
pictures going on in my mind, of a peep.

(DORIS *shakes her head.*)

It's the way you sit with your eyes down, lowered, that
recalls—(*little pause*) well, it recalls all the girls of the
village of my boyhood in Mayo, and none of the girls of
the lonely policeman's life in the city of London. (*Leans a
little closer.*) Are you one of those that likes to dance, now?

(DORIS *shakes her head.*)

Ah, but you'd be a natural dancer, I can see that, Doris,

44

not one of those that leads a man, you'd know enough to give in to him in his movements.

(*He leans a little closer. The door right, opens, and* MAY *comes out. Looks at* HAWKINS *and* DORIS, *crosses in front of them.*)

(*Straightening away from* DORIS): Ma'am. (*Nods, smiles.*)

(MAY *stares at him, goes on out through the door, right.*)

Now there's a lady would dance a man back out through the doors of the Mother Church herself. Doris Hoyden.

(*He looks at her.* DORIS *stares down into her lap.*)

I've got a great feeling about you, let me ask you now——

(*Stops, as the door right, opens and* MAY *comes back in, carrying a lavatory roll. Simultaneously* MR. GODBOY *comes out of the kitchen, carrying a glass of gin. He stares at* MAY *as she looks at* HAWKINS. MAY *continues across to the door, right.*)

GODBOY: Can I help, dear?

(MAY *slams the door.* MR. GODBOY *nods, smiles hands the glass to* HAWKINS, *sits down. There is a pause as* HAWKINS *drinks.*)

I think you was mentioning the gasser O'Higgs. (*Little pause, stares at* HAWKINS.) In relation to which, it's my own personal opinion that a man like O'Higgs prepared himself for the rope in the knowledge that it was going to go off ceremoniously without a hitch. To snatch the noose away from him with talk of specialists is to take the first step back into the jungle as far as I'm concerned. It puts an end to his heritage. (*Stares at him.*) May I say again Mannerly, what an honour it is to have you in my home at last while I'm on the subject. (*Little pause.*) Did you ever mingle with someone similar to O'Higgs, before the event, so to speak, socially?

HAWKINS: O'Higgs? The only O'Higgs I ever knew had the purest tenor voice in the whole world, you could hear that voice through the screams of the City of London itself. (*To* DORIS.) And what does your presently missing husband do, Doris, if I can ask?

DORIS (*after a pause*): He's between.

45

HAWKINS: Between?

GODBOY: Between jobs, she means. Eric's being a bit unlucky at the moment, through no fault of his own, naturally, as he's totally unqualified.

HAWKINS: But still there's a great luck if he has you to come home to, Doris, for that's what a marriage means. Has he been missing from you long?

(DORIS *shakes her head.*)

A little bit of night-wandering he goes in for, does he?

(DORIS *shrugs.*)

When the mood comes over him to count the stars of the sky and the blessings of his home? (*Laughs.*)

GODBOY: Eric is one of those who have—has—who succumbs to a weakish head for alcohol, I'm sorry to say.

HAWKINS (*to* DORIS): Well, he has a habit of turning up in the end, does he?

(DORIS *nods.*)

And that's a very pleasant habit for both of you, I think?

(DORIS *looks down. There is a long silence.* HAWKINS *stares at* DORIS, MR. GODBOY *stares at* HAWKINS.)

GODBOY: Inspector, may I be so bold as to show you something (*Gets up.*) It's merely this piece over here, a recent acquisition in a manner of speaking, for which I've got interesting plans.

(*As* HAWKINS *turns in his chair, goes to the cupboard.*)

Take a good look at it, sir, I'm particularly interested in your opinion.

(HAWKINS *leans over, pats* DORIS *on the knee.*)

(*Opens the cupboard door.*) I chose it myself. As you see, capacious. And around here, to the side, there's a hole, goodness only knows what for, Mannerly, originally.

(*Laughs, shakes his head, looks towards* HAWKINS, *who swings his head away from* DORIS.)

DORIS (*sidling down the couch*): Um, I've got to be um (*in a low voice. Gets up.*)

(HAWKINS *also gets up.*)

GODBOY: It's worth pointing out there's enough room to get a fully grown adult in here even May Godboy, my wife, could be got in here, sir. (*Laughs.*)

(DORIS *limps hurriedly to the door.* HAWKINS, *following
DORIS sidles ahead of her by the cupboard, so blocking
off her exit.*)

HAWKINS: It's big enough to get into you say? Now isn't that
amazing? (*To* DORIS.)

GODBOY: Indeed it is, sir. (*Gets into the cupboard.*) As I was
saying, capacious enough for May Godboy herself, who
could easily be accommodated.

HAWKINS (*as* DORIS *goes around the back of him, opens the door,
right*): May I just—for interest——?

(*He closes the cupboard door, holds it closed with his left
hand, catches* DORIS'S *hand with his right.*)

You're off upstairs then?

(DORIS *nods.*)

(*Stares at her.*) Well, perhaps we'll be seeing each other
again, some people I see over and over again, and there's
been a glimpse——

(*The door, left, opens and* MAY *comes out. Stops. Stares at*
HAWKINS, *who releases* DORIS'S *hand.*)

Good night, ma'am (*to* DORIS), and my respects to your
husband, I hope I'll be seeing him also.

(*As* DORIS *pulls away, stares at* MAY, *who shakes her head
knowingly, goes out of the room.* HAWKINS *turns, looks at*
MAY, *as knocking sounds come from within the cupboard.*)

(*There is a sudden blowing of whistles, yapping of dogs,
shouts, from a few streets distance.*)

(*To* MAY.) And there's Constable Hedderley calling.

MAY: Ooooh, everybody needs you so bad, don't they?
Including my husband, where is he?

HAWKINS: Ah! (*Opens the cupboard door.*) I'm off to Merrit
Street, Mr. Godboy, I'll wish you good night and thank
you. (*Leans in, shakes hands with* MR. GODBOY.)

GODBOY: Merrit Street! You've done it then! Congratulations,
Mannerly, congratulations, sir!

HAWKINS: Thank you, and good night.

(*Closes the cupboard door again, puts his hat on his head,
goes out, right. His voice in the hall——*)

47

All right, boys, all right, get moving boys, come on.
(*The front door bangs.* MAY *stands looking at the cupboard. It opens.* MR. GODBOY *steps out.*)

GODBOY: Merely, um . . . merely . . . something I wanted
Mannerly to see.
(MAY *shakes her head at him, then points her finger at her head, revolves it slowly.*)
Well, the Merrit Street attacker has been taken at last, dear.
(*Looks at her.*) I wonder whose trail Mannerly will be on
next, perhaps some time he'll be up against someone who
knows the game inside out, and can give him a real battle
of wits.

MAY: He's already on her trail, isn't he? And he'd have her
inside out before your eyes and you wouldn't know what
he was up to.

GODBOY: Pardon, dear?

MAY: Do you know what I've been doing in there?

GODBOY: What dear?

MAY: I've been telling you something.

GODBOY: Indeed dear? What?

MAY (*looks at him, goes over to the sofa, sits on it. She is now
wearing shoes*): What's the time?

GODBOY (*looks at his watch*): 10.30 bed-time, dear.

MAY: Come sit by me.

GODBOY (*stares at her*). Well, I noticed there was still—were
still some things in the cupboard, dear, I though we could
do it together.
(MAY *claps her hands, points to the floor beside her.* MR
GODBOY *comes over, sits down on the edge of the sofa,
gingerly, at* MAY's *feet.*)

MAY: You call that comfy?

GODBOY (*nods*): Thank you dear.

MAY: Well, I don't.
(*Gives him a push with her feet. He stumbles off the sofa.*)
Come on, let me have a last fling at your sad old head, as
that's the only part of you I'll remember as that's the only
part I'm allowed to touch. (*Points to the floor beside her.*)
(GODBOY *sits down on the floor, his head level with the sofa.*

48

*She starts to knead his head gently.*)

GODBOY: You've got a long night ahead of you. Tomorrow, I
merely mean, dear.

MAY: Oh shut up your niggidy-naggidy with your merely means.
(*Little pause.*) Rest easy now and settle yourself back,
because this is important. (*Slips her hand down his throat,
then begins to undo his tie.*) It's your last chance.

GODBOY: Pardon, dear?

MAY: The trouble with you is you won't let go, that's what's
defeating those specialists—if you've ever been to any.
(*Pulls his tie off.*) I got a lot of life in me yet, that's what I
been telling you, and if you'd just let me have a last-
minute go at you everything could still come right. (*Puts a
hand down his shirt, begins to rub his chest.*) There's a
lesson to be learnt with taking a high hand, we all want it
except for the freaks like Doris.

GODBOY: Doris, dear?

MAY: She won't give that boy what he needs. (*Shakes her head.*)
But there's some men could make us follow after them like
a wet puppy dog, and she'd better watch it, she's met her
match, from what I see of Hawkins. What's this doing to
you?

GODBOY: Making my chest nice and warm, thank you, dear.
Can I take you to mean that Doris and Eric's marriage is
definitely on a friendly type of basis?

MAY: She's not my idea of friendly, nor Eric's. And is *this*
doing you good?

GODBOY: Yes, dear, thank you, although not too warm, it tends
to tingle then—so Doris is against——

MAY: Tingle away, Number Two, tingle all over. Number One
used to like this more than anything.

GODBOY: Indeed, dear?

MAY: Oh you and Number One is poles apart, one always up,
two always down, and the horror of it is he's the one who's
dead. (*Little pause.*) Does it make you green to hear me
talk of Number One?

GODBOY: No dear, I enjoy hearing you reminisce.

(*There is a crash of the front door outside.* MR. GODBOY

*leaps to his feet, hurries over to the door, looks down the hall.*)

MAY: What is it?

GODBOY: It's Eric, dear. Eric.

(*Sound of feet in the hall, crashing.*)

Doris has been looking—what's happened to your trousers, Eric? (*Turns.*) He's gone.

MAY: What was the matter with him?

GODBOY: Nothing dear, except he looked out of breath and his trousers was—were torn.

MAY (*chuckles*): There's a boy after my own. If he's in the mood to do a bit of that on Doris, perhaps he'll save them both. (*Claps her hands, points to the floor.*)

(MR. GODBOY, *after a pause, comes back, sits down.*)

Don't it even make you green to see me having games with that Eric?

GODBOY: No dear, I particularly wanted you to have a pleasant evening, which was magnificently rounded off by the appearance of Inspector Hawkins himself.

MAY: Hawkins, O'Higgins, murder, wounds. I'd be better rubbing at a turtle. (*Removes her hand, lies still, stares at the ceiling.*) It's no go. No go. Last week it was my fiftieth birthday we was seeing out together and what did you do for it but spend the day creeping around them at the police station and the night sitting in your chair like a little white corpse. (*Long pause.*) I'm a warm woman, Perkins, everybody knows that, even your Manly Hawkins could see it in a wink, I'm a warm woman but the fire's going out. There's got to be hot coals to keep me banked, and you're turning me into embers, Perkins, embers. What'll happen to me if this goes on? What'll happen to me? (*There is a long silence.*) What do you say to me, then?

GODBOY: Dear. (*A pause. He sits staring ahead, his hands folded into his lap.*) If I haven't given satisfaction over the last two years, dear, it's because I've been waiting for me to see my path straight.

MAY: And do you see it straight to me, Perkins? (*Pause.*) Is that where the path's leading, into me?

50

GODBOY: No, dear. Now that Inspector Manly Hawkins has now called, after I'd given up all hope and was going to go ahead anyway, it can only lead to him, dear. (*Pause.*) I'm sorry.

MAY (*gets up. Stands looking down at him*): What do you want with him? He don't want anything from you, it's someone else *he's* after. (*Nods at ceiling.*)

GODBOY: And yet he came, dear, on time exactly. (*Looks up at her.*) To me.

MAY: Well, I don't care no more. That was a chance I was giving you, Perkins, and I wanted you to take it. Remember that, it's all I ask now. (*Goes to the large cupboard, flings it open, looks inside.*)

(MR. GODBOY *gets up, hurries over to the alcove, seizes the pipe, pulls it out, bends over, fishes for the cylinder, frantically pushes the pipe so that it falls into the guppie case, finds the cylinder, turns on the tap, drags the pipe out of the guppie case, turning around, as* MAY *steps out of the large cupboard, opens the door of the small cupboard, steps in.* MR. GODBOY *slams the door of the large cupboard, pushes the pipe through the hole and simultaneously jerks out the padlock, puts it through, closes it, turns back to the gas cylinder. As he is doing this,* MAY *steps out of the small cupboard, with a hat on her head, glances at* MR. GODBOY, *turns, stares at him, shakes her head, goes on into the room, left, reappears almost immediately with two suitcases, articles of clothing sticking out from under the lid, looks at* MR. GODBOY, *who is now pressed flat, stomach first, against the cupboard door. Shakes her head again, walks through the kitchen door.* MR. GODBOY *turns, his arms pressed back flat against the cupboard door.*)

GODBOY (*quietly*): Haw-kins. (*Staring blankly ahead.*)

CURTAIN

51

QUEEN MARGARET COLLEGE LIBRARY

## ACT TWO

### Scene 1

*The following afternoon.*

*The curtain rises on the same set as in Act One, but the room is now very neat.* MR. GODBOY *can be heard and partially seen in the kitchen, moving about. He comes fussily into the parlour with a new feather duster, which he flicks here and there. He is wearing an apron.*

*Suddenly he stops, stands alert, then puts the duster down and goes to the hall door, right. Stands listening, opens it a crack, peers out, opens it wider.*

GODBOY (*into the hall*): Doris.
> (*There is a little silence.*)
> I've just put the kettle on. (*Little pause—beckons with his hands.*)
> (DORIS *appears limping slightly more than in Act One. Her handbag is tightly clutched to her front. She stands at the door.*)
> I thought you'd forgotten, it looked as if you were passing me by. (*Laughs, ushers her in, makes to shut the door, is unable to do so. Opens it.*)

ERIC (*walks past him in a pair of bright new trousers*): Hello.

GODBOY (*stares at him for a long moment.* ERIC *stares back at him, confused*): Oh, you're coming in for a moment too, are you?

ERIC (*nods*): Yeah. (*Long pause.*) What? (*Short pause.*) Got old May off all right then, did you? (*Looks around.*) The place feels empty without her, eh Dorrie?
> (*Laughs nervously as* GODBOY *continues to stare at him.*)
> She certainly had a send-off from what we heard, eh Dorrie?

GODBOY (*walks briskly to the guppie case, sprinkles food on the*

*surface, puts a finger in, waggles it)*: Pardon, old boy?
(ERIC *watches him, then comes to stand beside him as* DORIS
*sits reluctantly on the sofa.*)

ERIC: You calling out good-byes to May.

GODBOY: Oh, pardon me for waking you, yes, I did shout after
her from the doorstep, I didn't mean to be heard. (*Puts the
package back on the table.*) There, there, my little fellows,
how's that for a feast?

ERIC (*looks at them closely*): Why they lying on top like that?

GODBOY: Because, old boy—(*stares a little closer*) they're dead.

ERIC: Oh, is that it.

(DORIS *lets out a little scream.*)

GODBOY (*picks one out, looks at it, drops it back in, wipes his
fingers on his apron*): This is very upsetting, I don't mind
admitting.

ERIC: How did it happen then?

GODBOY: Natural causes.

ERIC: Oh.

GODBOY: It can happen to anybody. Nevertheless it's a surprise.
It's the last thing I thought would happen.

(*There is a long silence.*)

DORIS (*who has been sniffing*): Gas.

GODBOY (*swings towards her*): Pardon, old boy?

DORIS: I smell gas.

GODBOY: No there isn't, old girl.

(*There is a pause.* ERIC *sniffs. Another pause.*)

ERIC: What is it then?

GODBOY: Merely a unfamiliar odour, old girl. (*Walking across
and taking off his apron.*) I've been boiling up some cabbage
heads. Perhaps it's merely that. (*Folds apron carefully, puts
it on the gramophone table.*)

ERIC: Can't help feeling sorry for them though. (*Puts his finger
into the water.*)

GODBOY: Indeed, that's only human. (*Goes over to* DORIS.) Well,
Doris, how are——?

ERIC: It's funny thinking of them, they was here last night
when we was clowning around enjoying ourselves, they was
swimming around then, back and forward and up and

53

down, and now today they're gone. Dead.

GODBOY (*listening, although facing* DORIS, *who is staring down into her lap*): Your husband Eric . . . (*with a smile*).

ERIC: Likely it was May's going did for them.

GODBOY (*turning*): You're talking nonsense, old boy, if you don't mind my speaking frankly to you as between friends, grief is unknown to fish.

ERIC: Is it? Oh?

(*As* GODBOY *turns back to* DORIS.)

What grief?

GODBOY: Pardon, old boy?

ERIC: What grief? You said grief.

GODBOY: I merely mean, old boy, that those guppies would hardly go away from grief of May's passing, pass away from grief of May's going I merely mean (*long pause*), and if you work it out, if they knew enough to know May was going away they'd know enough to know she was certainly coming back as far as she knew.

ERIC (*laughs*): Course they didn't know she wasn't coming back.

GODBOY (*nods his head at him several times*): I'm glad we're agreed on that, Eric. (*Turns back to* DORIS. *Stops. Turns back to* ERIC.) They didn't know she was going, I also mean.

ERIC: Oh. (*Nods vaguely.*)

GODBOY (*turning back to* DORIS): How's it coming along today, Doris?

ERIC: What will you do with them?

GODBOY: The remains will have to be disposed of, naturally, old boy. (*Little pause.*) What kind of trouble has it been causing you today, Doris?

DORIS: It's all right today.

GODBOY (*as* ERIC *comes across the room, and sits down in one of the utility chairs*): Really, Doris, my dear I was observing you closely as you limped across the room. We both know what needs doing to it. (*Turns to* ERIC.) Eh, Eric?

ERIC (*nods*): How will you dispose of the remains?

GODBOY: I will I will I will (*stops himself*). Pardon, old boy?

ERIC: Them gups.

GODBOY: They will have to be sluiced, old boy,

ERIC: Oh. Down the toilet you mean?

GODBOY (*nods*): Now Doris——

ERIC (*shaking his head*): Old May won't like that.

(GODBOY *stares at him.*)

No, she won't like having the remains sluiced, if I know May.

GODBOY: I wasn't talking about May's remains, I merely mean old boy, I was talking about the guppies' remains if you take my meaning? (*Turning his head quickly.*) I like your dress, Doris.

ERIC: What?

GODBOY: I was admiring Doris's dress.

ERIC: Oh? Where's my raincoat then?

GODBOY: Pardon?

ERIC: Well, wasn't it down here last night? (*Looks at* DORIS.)

GODBOY (*shakes his head. Stops shaking it as he remembers, then shakes it more vigorously*): It was not. No.

ERIC: Well, listen, me and May was having a dance and I was wearing it then, then me and May went into the kitchen for the stout and gin and I was wearing it then, then May come up to me and took it off me . . . (*looks around*) less she took it with her.

GODBOY: I don't mean to cause trouble, old boy, but May wouldn't be seen dead in that—in that—no, get that idea right out of your mind. (*Little pause.*) It'll turn up where you're least expecting it. (*Little pause.*) Righto, old boy?

ERIC: Oh. (*Nods.*) Righto.

GODBOY: Indeed you probably lost it when you went off in that strange way.

ERIC (*after a pause*): No, I wasn't wearing it then, no.

GODBOY: Where did you go anyway, we all sat here worrying about you.

ERIC: Oh. (*Laughs, hunches a shoulder.*) Out. I went out.

GODBOY: Yes, well Doris was in a state, it needed Inspector Hawkins himself to calm her down.

(*There is a long pause.*)

ERIC: What was he doing here?

GODBOY: Merely visiting myself, old boy.

ERIC: Oh. (*Nods.*) You haven't seen my scarf then?
> (GODBOY *stares at him coldly. There is a long silence.*)
> (*Looks around him, stares at the cupboard, points at it*): *I know, I. . . .*

GODBOY: Now I don't mean to cause offence (*shouting*) but I'm getting tired of all these accusations of scarves and raincoats and sluicing May down the toilet, that is the guppies, where's your manners?
> (*Long pause.* ERIC *stares at him in bewilderment,* DORIS *stares down into her lap.*)
> Do I get my apology?
> (ERIC *shakes his head perplexed. There is another pause.*)

DORIS (*in a whisper*): Say pardon.

ERIC: Oh. Righto. Pardon.

GODBOY (*nods*): Least said, soonest mended, old boy.
> (*He gets up, goes into the kitchen, leaving door open.* ERIC *looks at* DORIS, *who keeps her face bent. He looks away.*)

ERIC (*finally crossing his legs, begins to jog a foot up and down, whistles tunelessly.* DORIS *glares at him. He stops. Pause. Looks at her She looks away*): Honest, Dorrie, I was just walking.

DORIS: Walking!

ERIC: Just walking around, that's all.

DORIS (*in a hiss*): And what about me, with that policeman, what was I meant to be doing while you was just walking around, with him walking around me. And them trousers you caught on barbed wire. What barbed wire?

ERIC: Well, I told you, there was this barbed wire——
> (DORIS *turns her face away.*)
> Anyway, you heard him, that policeman was just visiting.
> (*Looks at* DORIS's *face.*) I love you, Dorrie.
> (DORIS *pays no attention.*)
> (ERIC *sits hunched. Begins to jog his foot again, looks around the room hopelessly, sees cupboard, gets up, goes over to it, stares at it closely, then tries handle. Pulls harder, then holds up the padlock.*)
> Here, Dorrie!
> (*She pays no attention. He peers between the door crack, gets*

*down on one knee.* GODBOY *comes into the room carrying a tray. Puts tray down on the floor, picks up two cups, carries one to* DORIS, *puts it beside her.*)

GODBOY: Sugar, my dear?

DORIS: Yes please.

GODBOY: What about Eric? Eric?

ERIC: Yes, please. (*Peering now with his face close to the crack.*)

GODBOY (*stirs* DORIS'S *cup for her*): There. Lots of sugar to sweeten your outlook on things. (*Chuckles, pats her shoulder.*) Not to worry, Doris. Not to worry. (*Nods, turns, walks across the room with* ERIC'S *cup, puts it down on the floor beside him, turns, walks eagerly back towards* DORIS.) It's worrying does more harm than corns and ulcers put— (*stops. Turns, looks at* ERIC.) Old boy?

ERIC: Yeah. (*Sniffing hard.*)

GODBOY: Haven't you got any respect, old boy? Haven't you got any? Any respect?

ERIC: What? (*Turns his head.*) What for?

GODBOY: For—for—for property, I merely mean.

ERIC: Oh.

(*Looks at* DORIS, *gets up. Stares at* GODBOY, *who is glaring at him.*)

DORIS (*after a long pause*): Say pardon, Eric.

ERIC: Oh. Righto. Pardon.

(*Little pause, as* GODBOY *nods slowly.*)

GODBOY: Granted, Eric, as soon as asked. Now—(*gestures to one of the chairs.*)

ERIC: But I thought May said it was for us.

GODBOY: Indeed it is.

ERIC: Oh. (*Comes back to his chair. Sits down.*) But it's locked.

GODBOY (*about to sit down, pauses*): Indeed it is.

ERIC (*looks at* DORIS): Well——?

GODBOY: It'll have to remain locked until further notice, thank you for reminding me.

ERIC: Oh. (*Looks at* DORIS *again.*) But I remember see, that's where I put my scarf and raincoat, see.

GODBOY (*strikes his knee*): How many times do I have to tell you. (*Shouting.*) There's nothing in there except May's remains.

57

(*Long pause. They all sit staring ahead.*)
By which I merely mean the bits and pieces of May
(*falters*) which she couldn't take with her and had to leave
behind. (*Little pause.*) If you take my meaning, old boy.
(*Little pause.*) Have you got those facts straight in your
mind?

ERIC: Righto, yes, righto. Pardon.

GODBOY (*after a pause*): Granted.

(*There is a long silence. They drink their tea.* DORIS *with her
head lowered,* GODBOY *genteely,* ERIC *from the wrong side of
the cup.*)

(*To* DORIS.) Excuse me speaking sharpish to your husband,
I don't mean you to take it personally. (*To* ERIC.) It's just
at the rate he's going on funny things will be turning up all
over my parlour. (*Laughs.*)

ERIC *laughs. There is another long silence.*

ERIC: This cupboard then, that's got all this stuff of May's in it
and it's locked, are you still giving it to us then?

GODBOY: Indeed I am, yes, the sooner you get it up to your
own parlour the happier I'll be.

ERIC: Oh. (*Nods.*) Well (*looks at* DORIS) that's a bit funny, well,
I mean (*laughs, looks at* DORIS), you're giving us this
cupboard and it's got May's stuff in it, and it's locked up
so we can't get into it anyway, and it'll take up all the
room in our room won't it? And I mean that's a bit funny.
As we can't get into it even.

(GODBOY *looks at him, goes over to the cupboard, bends
down, opens the drawers at the base, turns, folds his arms,
looks at* ERIC.)

(ERIC *looks at* DORIS, *who looks away.*)

GODBOY (*quietly*): Any further complaints, Eric?

(ERIC *shrugs.*)

(GODBOY *comes back, sits down, sips from his tea.*)

(ERIC *looks at him, looks at* DORIS, *looks at him again.
Laughs suddenly.*)

(GODBOY *puts his cup into its saucer, stares at* ERIC.)

ERIC: No, I was just laughing because it's a bit funny getting a
cupboard you can't get into except in a bottom drawer and

58

it's as big as our room nearly and it's ponging away.
That's all.
(*Pause, while* GODBOY *looks at him,* DORIS *looks down into her cup.*)
Well, you smell it, Dorrie. Go on, smell it.

GODBOY (*folds his arms*): Doris, be a good girl and smell it, will you Doris? As that's what your husband wants.

DORIS (*gets up, limps across the room, smells the cupboard, limps back*): It's not too bad. (*In a low voice, looks accusingly at* ERIC.)

GODBOY: Virtually odour free?

DORIS: I smelt far worse from that leak we had in the stove.

GODBOY: Thank you, Doris. (*To* ERIC.) Well, old boy? (*Little pause.*) Eric?

ERIC: Um. (*Looks from* DORIS *to* GODBOY.) It's just that it smells funny to me. Gas in a cupboard. (*Little pause.*) It smells funny.

GODBOY: Oh does it old boy, and if it does I'll tell you why, it's because you're turning a bit nosey, frankly speaking. Righto. (*Little pause.*) Righto.

ERIC (*after a pause*): Pardon.

GODBOY: Granted as asked. Now to change the subject to something pleasant, did you hear the news about Inspector Mannerly Hawkin's success in the Merrit Street case. He was here last night, wasn't he Doris, just prior to catching the man who's certainly helping him now down at the station, if I know Mannerly Hawkins. (*Laughs.*) Eh, Doris?

ERIC: Oh? (*Laughs.*) I heard something about that, yes. (*Looks around the room, begins to jog his leg.*)

GODBOY: Yes, if you hadn't run off like that, you could have met Mannerly too, Eric. Still, May and Doris met him, I'm glad about that. Eh, Doris? (*Smiles at her.*) He's got amazing instincts, Mannerly has. (*Turns to* ERIC.) What did you hear?

ERIC: Nothing, no. (*Shakes his head.*) Only when I was down at the um, 'bacanist's there was something I heard about this girl undoing her stockings or something and this chap went up to her, or something like that.

DORIS: When did you go down to the 'bacanist's?

GODBOY (*laughs*): That was no girl, Eric, that was Police Constable Hedderley.

ERIC: Who?

GODBOY: Hawkins' female accomplice, old boy.

ERIC (*angrily*): What was she doing there, then?

GODBOY: Pardon?

ERIC: Well, what was she taking her stockings off for then?

GODBOY: Bait, Eric, she was bait in the trap.

ERIC: Well, what'll happen to him, then?

GODBOY: Further promotion. Or another favourable mention from a judge.

ERIC: No, this bloke. The one you say they um. . . .

GODOBY: With Mannerly Hawkins on the job, Eric?

ERIC: But suppose they get—got—I mean it's the wrong bloke?

GODBOY: I repeat, Eric—we're talking about Inspector Mannerly Hawkins.

ERIC (*thinks*): Well, but if he was a bloke coming home from going into the air to clear his brain for a moment, and happened to be in the area by mistake, see, and there was this girl pulling her stockings off and waving them at him, this—um, bloke he might come up to her, just from—well, and asked what she was doing larking about and if his brain was a bit fogged she could have got hold of him and pitched him to the ground bruising his shoulder something —see what I mean, it could be an accident, see. (*Long pause.*) No, I'm thinking, that's all. (*Little pause.*) No.

GODBOY: I say it again, Eric (*laughs*), we're talking about Inspector Mannerly Hawkins. Down there at the station he's dealing with a criminal second in value to a murderer himself. Mannerly doesn't make mistakes, Eric, as I ought to know.

ERIC: Oh. (*Little pause.*) That's all right then. (*Little pause.*) I mean if he's got someone he thinks did it, and he doesn't make mistakes, that's all right then. He can't grumble.

GODBOY: Who can't grumble?

ERIC: This chap they got.

GODBOY: Oh, he'll grumble all right, there's very few know how to help the police, Eric, very few like the gasser O'Higgs. After he'd been trapped with the corpse of his wife in an airing-closet, and the female tenant laid out on the kitchen table, stark, he knew his time was come. He sat down and wrote out a brilliant confession on the spot. Being in a lawyer's office he knew the language. There's very few men like O'Higgs, and an animal like the Merrit Street attacker wouldn't be one of them.

(DORIS *shudders.*)

What is it, Doris?

DORIS: I been having dreams about him, nightmares I mean.

ERIC (*looks at her, clears his throat*): Who?

DORIS: Him. People like him. The one was in Merrit Street.

(ERIC *gets up, takes his cup over to the record table, then wanders to the guppie case, stops in front of it, peers in, turns, wanders towards the cupboard, stops in front of it, raps on the door, stops himself, looks towards* GODBOY *furtively, then stands by the cupboard listening to the conversation between* DORIS *and* GODBOY.)

GODBOY: What sort of nightmares would those be, Doris?

DORIS: I mean, what could you do, if he got you? What could you do? And people, what would they think? There was one I was reading about in the States of America, he did things to girls with tape and shoe laces and stuffed their mouths with cotton-wool so the girls was helpless, and was powerless to struggle, and then he did other things to them. It wasn't their fault.

GODBOY (*as* ERIC *abstractedly opens the bottom drawer of the cupboard, begins to unwind the length of pipe*): No Doris, if you were rendered incapable first, you'd be cleared of any blame.

DORIS: And when I was little there was this one he used to wait at bus-stops in his car, he was after us when we was little.

GODBOY: They're different, Doris. There's no excuse for that. I hope the authorities realize hanging's too good for them, what they need is medical treatment from specialists.

DORIS: But this Merrit Street one, he couldn't come through my bedroom window when I was all asleep and quiet, and done

61

things to me, he could've bound me up and I couldn't have done nothing if he did it by force, while you (*to* ERIC) was walking the streets.

ERIC (*shakes his head*): Not to you, Dorrie, I wouldn't do that.

GODBOY (*looks towards him, leaps to his feet*): Now Eric what you prying into how, Eric?

ERIC: Well, it was in this drawer. (*Holds out the cylinder.*) It's got that gas smell to it.

GODBOY (*walking across to him*): Smell, smell, smell, all you talk about is smell. (*Takes the cylinder away from* ERIC, *thrusts it behind the alcove curtain.*) Now I'll tell you, old boy, I'm getting tired of telling you your manners in front of your own wife, you're interrupting a very pleasant conversation we're having. (*Turns, looks him in the face, very close.*) And there's another thing, old boy, what are your plans for the afternoon?

ERIC: What?

GODBOY: Because frankly, old boy, it's time Doris and me were getting down to it—her corn I merely mean, and it's medically a trifle funny to have a patient's husband loitering about in my cupboards. (*Long pause.*) What about going to the pictures?

(ERIC *looks at* DORIS.)

DORIS (*looking down into her handbag*): Could we do it tomorrow?

GODBOY: No Doris, I'm sorry to say I've got to get you over with, any moment now my time might not be my own.

DORIS: Well (*hesitates*), can't he stay then?

GODBOY: Again I have to say no, Doris, on general grounds. This is between you and me, my dear. (*Looks at her, then takes* ERIC *by the arm, leads him to the door, right.*) Now you go to the pictures, then you stroll about a bit, and then you look in on me, it'll be all over then as far as Doris is concerned, I merely mean we'll have had it off. (*Little pause.*) Righto?

ERIC: Oh. (*Shrugs.*) Well.

(*Looks at* DORIS, *walks past* GODBOY, *kisses* DORIS. *She turns her mouth away.*)

Well ta-ta, Dorrie.

DORIS (*in a low voice*): Ta-ta.

(GODBOY *ushers him out of the room, stares after him,
watched by* DORIS, *then shuts the door. Stands looking at*
DORIS. *There is a pause. He comes and sits by her on the
sofa, folds his hands into his lap, clears his throat.* DORIS
*looks down at her handbag.*)

GODBOY (*after a little pause*): How are you feeling now, Doris?

DORIS: Cold. I feel cold.

GODBOY: Cold, eh? That's a good sign.

DORIS: Is it?

GODBOY: It's when people get all heated up that inconveniences
begin.

DORIS: Oh. (*Little pause.*) Can I have the fire on, then?

GODBOY (*leaps to his feet*): Indeed my—(*sits down again*). No,
I'm sorry to say that might be a trifle risky under the
circumstances. (*Long pause.*) Because of the little whiff I
might be compelled to give you.

DORIS (*after a long pause*): What for?

GODBOY: It's usual in these cases, Doris. (*Laughs.*) Never you
mind your little head about that, dear.
(*There is a long silence.* GODBOY *turns his head and stares
at* DORIS.)
I'm sorry about my treatment of Eric, he's a good lad.
Above all, most likeable. (*Little pause.*) What was it
precisely that attracted you about him?

DORIS: Well, it was that he looks like that Humphrey Bogart.

GODBOY: Oh, indeed my dear, you do surprise me there, my
own impression of Humphrey Bogart on one viewing is of
a trifle more educated man. But these things are a matter
of personal taste.

DORIS: It's when he wears his raincoat.

GODBOY: His raincoat isn't in this room, Doris.
(*Long pause.*)

DORIS: Whiff of what?

GODBOY: Pardon?

DORIS: Whiff of something, you said.

GODBOY: Indeed. (*Nods.*) My own marriage to May was a
blessing in its way. I didn't know what it was I wanted

63

until I met her and found myself thinking about it. Fifty years a bachelor is a long time for a man, he dreams of what he is but he don't—doesn't do anything about it until fate compels him. (*Looks at* DORIS.) I've followed Mannerly Hawkins' career since the moment I saw him, down at the self-same station he's returned to. There was something there that bound us together, Doris. Did you know O'Higgs was taken into custody by a man he'd worked with in his capacity as a lawyer's clerk. He addressed some letters to him, personal letters, from his final cell. They were eventually published in a newspaper.

(*Long pause.*)

DORIS (*clears her throat*): Whiff of what, will it be?

GODBOY (*looks at her*): Whiff of the same thing I had to give to May, Doris. (*Little pause.*) If it hadn't been for my wound, things would have been different. I'd have been a different man on the force. Mannerly Hawkins is a man. He's got the authority.

(*Pause.*)

DORIS: It's funny. (*Laughs.*) It's not hurting me now.

(GODBOY *looks at her again, bends towards her, pats her on the arm, gets up, arranges one of the utility chairs so that it's facing to the left. He goes to the alcove, takes out a cardboard box.* DORIS *watches. He comes back, clears his throat, stands holding the back of the arranged chair. Bends over, pats the seat with his hand.* DORIS *watches. Pats the seat again. Laughs.* DORIS *limps over, sits down.* GODBOY *squares his shoulders, turns, stands behind* DORIS.)

GODBOY: Kindly remove the shoe and stocking please. (*Stiffly, then turns around and folds his arms over his chest.*)
(DORIS *slowly takes off her shoe, then her stocking.*)
Ready?

DORIS (*in a low voice*): Yes.

GODBOY (*walks stiffly around the chair*): Would you mind just stretching it out, Doris, so I can have a proper glimpse of it.
(DORIS *stretches her leg out.*)
(GODBOY *crouches down some distance from the foot, inspects it carefully. After a little pause, whistles.*)

64

(DORIS *looks at him in alarm.*)

We just got to it in time. It's burgeoning fast. There'll be danger if it's allowed to develop. (*Gets up, goes to the alcove, picks out a box from the back, then another one. Comes back, opens the top box, takes out small knives, pads, lotions, puts them on the floor.*) I've been a great admirer of yours, Doris. I expect you realize that.

DORIS (*watching him*): What?

GODBOY: We share similar ideas about things, Doris, very similar. (*Stares up at her.*) I appreciate what you was— were telling me about your dreams. (*Gets up, holding the second box.*) As I said to May, violence to a living creature isn't in my nature. That's why I was a bachelor for fifty years. (*Opens the box.*) Now I have to administer a whiff of something mild.

DORIS: Well (*in a shaky voice*), what is it?

GODBOY: It's to help you out.

DORIS (*shakes her head*): I don't want that.

GODBOY: Now Doris, I wouldn't want to have myself having to counter serious opposition. There could be dangerous responses made by your reflexes which could throw me off my stride. (*Laughs.*) It's a case of too many cooks can spoil the broth, merely.

(*He comes around to stand beside* DORIS. *She looks up at him. There is a long silence.*)

You won't give me any trouble, will you, Doris?

(DORIS *shakes her head.*)

(*Puts a hand on her shoulder.*) Thank you, Doris.

DORIS: What's that, then?

GODBOY: This. (*Holds the box up.*) This will make you laugh when you see it. (*Little pause.*) I'll have to ask you to slip it on in a minute of your own volition. It's facilitate matters dreadfully for you.

DORIS (*makes a ghastly laughing sound*): But what is it?

GODBOY: It's an appliance you're familiar with. It'll even bring back childhood memories. I've done some alterations so that it comes in handy for what's got to be done. My own invention. (*Opens the box, shows her the contents, laughs.*)

E

(DORIS *stares down into it.*)

Righto?

(DORIS *shakes her head, starts to get up.*)

(*Pressing her down with his hand.*) Righto.

(DORIS *subsides. Sits staring down into her lap. He comes round so that his back is to the audience, blocking her from view. There are slight struggling sounds. He keeps his back to the audience.*)

There you are, it's the right size, it suits perfectly.

(DORIS *makes mumbling sounds.*)

(*Stands stiffly for a moment, puts his hands behind his back, twists them, his head up. Then bends.*) You look as right as rain.

(DORIS *mumbles.*)

(*Shouting.*) You look as right as rain.

(*Little pause, further mumbling from* DORIS.)

As *rain*, I said.

(*Sounds of footsteps in the hall, right.*)

ERIC (*shouting*): I know, and I haven't got my raincoat.

GODBOY (*stands frozen by the chair. There is a pause, then tentatively*): Pardon?

ERIC: Dorrie!

GODBOY: What do you want?

ERIC: It looks like rain, and I need my raincoat, that's all.

GODBOY: It isn't here. I told you.

ERIC: Oh. (*Pause.*) How's it going then?

GODBOY: Doris is in excellent condition. (*Holding her shoulders as she struggles to rise.*)

ERIC: I'll be off to the pictures then.

GODBOY: Righto.

(*Sound of* ERIC *moving about outside the door, then a confusion of steps.*)

(GODBOY *hurries over to the door, right exposing* DORIS *for the first time. She is wearing a gasmask. He opens the door, right, stares down the hall then closes the door, turns the key in the lock. As he is doing this the door left opens, and* ERIC *puts his head in. Stares at* DORIS *as* GODBOY *steps away from the door, turns, sees him. There is a long pause.*)

66

ERIC: What you doing in that, then? (*To* DORIS, *bursts out laughing*.)

(DORIS *makes mumbling sounds*.)

GODBOY (*hurries back, puts a hand on* DORIS'*s arm*): You're interrupting a very important moment, Eric. This is no time for your jokes.

ERIC (*stops laughing. Looks grave. Lets out another snort. Stops*): I'm going to see *Flame and Arrow* with that Virgin Mayo and Burt Lancaster. (*Little pause*.) That all right?

(DORIS *stares at him*.)

*Flame and Arrow*. (*Bellows. Pantomimes drawing a bow*.)

(DORIS *nods*.)

(*To* GODBOY.) It's outlaws in the woods. She don't like them, she likes cities. (*Little pause*.) It's where he catches her and keeps her chained by a chain around her neck. (*There is a little pause*.) It'll be good. (*Little pause*.) Righto. (*Little pause*.) Ta ta then.

GODBOY: Ta ta.

(ERIC *walks across the stage to the door, right, watched by* GODBOY, *tries the handle, finds it locked, steps away, comes back across the stage*.)

ERIC: Righto.

(GODBOY, *who has kept a hand on* DORIS'*s shoulder, hurries after* ERIC *with a utility chair, puts it under the handle. Comes back, looks at* DORIS, *pats her on the shoulder. Goes to the alcove, takes out gas cylinder, length of pipe, starts to come back. There is a knock on the door, right. He turns angrily, puts the cylinder down, goes to the door, right. Puts his ear against it. Sound of footsteps*.

GODBOY (*shouting*): I'm beginning to think your Eric is a trifle mad, Doris. If you'll pardon me for saying so. (*Unlocks door, opens it a fraction, peers out, opens it wider, then steps out of sight into the hall as the door, left, opens inwards, thus causing the chair to fall over*.)

(HAWKINS *enters, followed by* HEDDERLEY, *in a long police skirt, tunic, curls, etc*.)

HAWKINS (*stares down at* DORIS, *as* HEDDERLEY *takes up a position by the record table, hands behind back*): Well, and

67

here's a pretty sight. (*Laughs.*)

(DORIS *stares up at him, then down into her lap as* GODBOY *comes back in through the door, left, stepping carefully over the chair. Stops. Stares at* HAWKINS.)

GODBOY: So you've come again! (*Reverently.*)

HAWKINS: I think we're interrupting something, Mr. Godboy.

GODBOY (*as* HAWKINS *turns back to* DORIS): No Mannerly, no. Please pardon the mess.

(*Goes to the door, left, picks up the chair,* HAWKINS *is now staring down at* DORIS'*s leg. She draws it up awkwardly, sits with her hands clasped around her handbag.*)

We was—were just about to get commencing down to a nastyish business. (*Little pause.*) Doris's corn, I merely mean. (*Comes back, picks up the cylinder, carries it, with the tube trailing behind, to the alcove*) and a preliminary settling down I go in for as part of my technique. (*Comes back.*) Doris is a nervous girl (*bends over her*) so I slipped this on in a reminiscent vein about the old days. (*In a low voice, takes the gasmask off.*)

(DORIS *looks around, looks down at her handbag.*)

HAWKINS: Ah, and so it's you, Doris Hoyden. (*Crouches slightly to stare at her.*) But you're not still waiting for the wandering husband? (*Little pause.*) He wouldn't still be on the wander now?

GODBOY: He's just gone this second, Mannerly.

HAWKINS (*looks at* HEDDERLEY): Now isn't that a pity, then.

(HEDDERLEY *nods.*)

(*There is a pause.* GODBOY *walks over to the alcove, the gasmask in his hands.*)

GODBOY: I'm merely, um, pardon me. . . .

HAWKINS: Mr. Godboy.

(GODBOY *stops, turns.*)

(*Comes towards him, revolving his hat in his hand. Stands thoughtfully for a moment, then puts his hand on* GODBOY'*s left shoulder.* GODBOY *comes to attention, as if under arrest. Then* HAWKINS *moves to the cupboard, gives the padlock a flick.*)

Ah, and it's quite a lock you've locked your treasures up

with. (*Turns, smiles at* GODBOY.)

(DORIS, *during this, picks up her shoe and stocking and begins to limp towards the kitchen door.*)

(*Quietly, still smiling at* GODBOY.) Hedderley.

(HEDDERLEY *shifts around, stands beside* DORIS. DORIS *stops.* HEDDERLEY *stares at the side of her face.* DORIS *is facing the wall, right.*)

GODBOY: Yes, sir. (*Little pause.*) Unfortunately I can't put my hand on the key at this precise moment, Mannerly, which has got itself unfortunately lost somehow.

HAWKINS (*turns, looks down at the guppies*): And the charming Mrs. Godboy?

GODBOY: Unfortunately May Godboy is no longer with us just at the moment, I'm sorry to say. She took that trip I was hinting about last night.

HAWKINS: Did she now. (*Puts his finger into the water.*) Not as sprightly as yesterday, I think.

GODBOY (*after a pause*): A little run down, and in need of a rest, now you ask, Mannerly.

HAWKINS (*still staring into the tank*): Not dead though?

GODBOY: No Mannerly. . . . It's a kind of holiday.

HAWKINS: A holiday. (*Stirs his fingers around.*) How strange the littlest creatures are, in their ways. How strange.

GODBOY (*after a pause, laughs*): Very true, Mannerly, very true.

HAWKINS: Mr. Godboy. (*Looks at him.*) What it is, Mr. Godboy, is that there's a little matter we're trying to get to the bottom of.

GODBOY: Sir?

HAWKINS (*comes over, puts a hand on* GODBOY's *shoulder again*): And I think you can help us, Mr. Godboy.

GODBOY (*stares into his face*): Help you in your inquiries, Mannerly. Yes, sir.

(*There is a long pause.*)

Do you want me to accompany you to the station, Mannerly?

HAWKINS (*shakes him gently by the shoulder*): Well, to tell you the truth, we're on a little game of cat and mouse, and sometimes it's better for the cat to sit beneath the mouse's lair. (*Tilts his head, smiles.*) Isn't that the truth?

GODBOY: I've been expecting another visit, Mannerly, but I didn't expect even you would be precisely—(*shakes his head in admiration*). May I say, whatever the outcome of your present inquiries, my congratulations are offered again on your Merrit Street attacker triumph. It will always be an honour, wherever I may end up, to recall that you sat in one of my chairs while it was happening. It'll be mentioned in my letters, Mannerly, from wherever I end up.
(HAWKINS *is looking towards* HEDDERLEY *and* DORIS *throughout this.*)
And of course similarly congratulations to Constable Hedderley, if that is Constable Hedderley that is.

HAWKINS: That is. Although Hedderley's a little modest about accepting congratulations this morning, aren't you now, Hedderley?

HEDDERLEY: Sir.

GODBOY: Even so, the Merrit Street attacker's a big feather to have had in her cap.

HAWKINS (*laughs, shakes his head, walks towards the centre of the room followed by* MR. GODBOY, *still clutching the gas-mask*): Hedderley wouldn't know how to receive a feather like that, would you, Hedderley? Your whole nature's against it, isn't it, Hedderley?

HEDDERLEY: Sir.

GODBOY (*after a pause, looking from* HAWKINS *to* HEDDERLEY *and* DORIS): That's in the best tradition, sir, of course. If I may say so personally, I think it's wonderful that the fair sex is being taken up, as long as they're not in it for the glamour merely of course.

HAWKINS: Hedderley?

HEDDERLEY: Sir.

HAWKINS: Did you hear what Mr. Godboy said about the fair sex? Are you in it for the glamour?

HEDDERLEY: Sir. (*Shakes head.*)

GODBOY (*after a long pause, during which* HAWKINS *looks towards* HEDDERLEY, *who continues to stare at the side of* DORIS's *face*): Of course, even with the fair sex good officers are born and not made.

HAWKINS: Well, Hedderley, how would you answer Mr. Godboy on that? Were you born, do you think, Hedderley, or were you made?

HEDDERLEY: Sir. (*Little pause.*) Made, sir.

HAWKINS: By whom were you made then, Hedderley?

HEDDERLEY: Sir. (*Little pause.*) By sir, sir.

HAWKINS (*turns, smiles at* MR. GODBOY, *tilts his head, turns back to* HEDDERLEY): Now fill me in, Hedderley, on what you're doing at the moment?

HEDDERLEY: Sir. Nothing, sir.

HAWKINS: Well then, ask the young lady to turn around, it's rude to keep her on edge like that.

((HEDDERLEY *says something in a low voice to* DORIS, *who turns around slowly, clasping her handbag, her shoe and her stocking to her waist.*)

(*Goes up to her.*) Excuse our manners, Doris Hoyden, why don't you make yourself comfortable?

(*Gestures to the sofa.* DORIS *looks at him, limps over to the sofa, sits in its corner, tightly.*)

No, no, Doris, right in the middle, the middle of the sofa's the most comfortable.

(DORIS *shifts to the middle.* HEDDERLEY *looks at* HAWKINS, *who tilts head almost imperceptibly.* HEDDERLEY *sits down next to* DORIS, *on* DORIS'*s left.* HAWKINS *turns one of the utility chairs around and straddles it, facing the other utility chair, which, after a hesitation,* MR. GODBOY *turns around and also straddles.* HAWKINS *begins to revolve his hat in his hands.* HEDDERLEY *takes* DORIS'*s handbag from her, opens it, begins to go through it.* DORIS *sits staring down into her lap.* MR. GODBOY *begins to revolve the gasmask in his hands. There is a silence.*)

GODBOY: So you're already on the trail of something else, Mannerly, after last night? (*Laughs.*)

HAWKINS: Ah (*shakes his head*) it's not all the city's wickedness happens at night, Mr. Godboy, as you'd be knowing yourself, I think. (*Stares at him.*) There's a loneliness that comes with day-break that can turn a man's heart in his chest, isn't there? And fog his mind with the sorrow of us all.

GODBOY: Indeed, Mannerly? (*Staring back at him, revolving the gasmask in time to* HAWKINS' *revolutions.*)

HAWKINS: The evil's done by day-break, Mr. Godboy. The morning has its own cries, and who can hear them if a policeman can't? How can a city live, if a city's lost its faith, and has its horrors locked in its households.

GODBOY (*as* HEDDERLEY *opens* DORIS'*s compact, tastes its contents*): I can assure you, Mannerly, that key will turn up eventually.

HAWKINS: No, Mr. Godboy, the key was thrown away by the fathers of the nation. (*Rubs his eyes.*) There's not the difference I used to think, when I was in the care of the real fathers, between the vocation of the priest and the vocation of the policeman. We're both of us lonely from discipline. (*Laughs.*) And who is there, in this city, can tell them apart, the sinners and the sufferers, if the policeman can't?

GODBOY (*confused*): There's no doubt that you can, Mannerly, your record shows it.

HAWKINS (*leans over, takes* DORIS'*s stocking from her lap, runs his hands along it, his hat on his knee*): But if loneliness can sour men into sinners, it's discipline can convert sinners into policemen. (*Begins to knot the stocking.*) Would there be something in the house can ease my throat from its preaching? (*Laughs.*)

(GODBOY *stares at him, puzzled.*)

A little drop of whatever it was you found for me last night, but only if you've got some.

GODBOY: Indeed, Mannerly. (*Little pause.*) Gin?

HAWKINS: Whatever it was, water and something or other, I think.

(GODBOY *gets up, goes into the kitchen.*)

(*Turns to* HEDDERLEY *and* DORIS): Hedderley?

HEDDERLEY: Sir?

HAWKINS: Are you going through Mrs. Hoyden's handbag, Hedderley? Is that what I'm seeing?

HEDDERLEY: Sir.

HAWKINS: And did you give Hedderley permission, Doris?

72

(DORIS *shakes her head.*)

Well—and why don't you ask what Hedderley's up to then, as is your right?

(DORIS *looks down, shakes her head.*)

Ask anyway.

DORIS (*in a whisper*): It's all right.

HAWKINS (*who has knotted the stocking several times, leans forward, letting it hang from his hand*): Ask Hedderley, Doris.

DORIS (*in a whisper*): Why are you looking through my handbag? (HEDDERLEY *hands it back to* DORIS.)

HAWKINS (*to* DORIS): Demand an apology, Doris. (*Pause.*) Doris. (*Little pause.*) Doris.

DORIS (*in a whisper*): Say pardon.

HEDDERLEY (*after a pause*): Sorry, m'am.

HAWKINS (*gets up, sits down on the right of* DORIS, *stares at her intently, as he unknots the stocking*): Doris, it's slipped my mind, what did you say your foot-loose husband's name was, Doris?

DORIS (*in a whisper*): Eric.

HAWKINS (*glances at* HEDDERLEY, *who shakes her head imperceptibly*): That's right, and that's it. (*Little pause, puts hand on* DORIS'*s knee.*) Between-Jobs Eric. (*Laughs, tilts his head.*) And tell me, Doris, aren't you perhaps suffering from loneliness with Between-Jobs always going away from you like that?

(DORIS *shakes her head,*)

So you're expecting him back, then, sometime between now and never?

DORIS (*as* MR. GODBOY *comes into the room, with a glass with water in it, and a bottle of gin*): He'll be back for tea, he said.

(GODBOY *hands the glass to* HAWKINS, *who looks at* HEDDERLEY, *abstractedly takes the bottle from* MR. GODBOY, *who is just about to pour, and pours himself a large gin.*)

HAWKINS: For tea?

GODBOY: Eric's a bit funny in his movements, but he's not one to forget his tummy, I'll say that for him.

HAWKINS (*swallows from his drink*): As long as you don't prefer
him gone, Doris, and send word to him to stay away?
(*Squeezes her knee with his other hand, laughs, tilts his
head at her.*)
(DORIS *shakes her head.*)
Ah, but then you'd be having a mother to turn to, if you
felt lost beyond yourself?
(DORIS *shakes her head.*)
And no father either?
(DORIS *shakes her head.*)
(*Drinks some more, his hand still on* DORIS's *knee.*) Ah, and
Hedderley's in the way of being an orphan too, aren't you,
Hedderley?

HEDDERLEY: Sir.

HAWKINS: Which is why Hedderley took to the discipline of the
policehood, isn't it Hedderley? (*Laughs.*)

HEDDERLEY: Sir.

HAWKINS (*tilts his head, laughs*): Ah, there's been a glimpse,
Doris. Somewhere. I know it.
(HAWKINS *hands the glass back to* MR. GODBOY, *gets up,*
HEDDERLEY *also gets up. Looks down at* DORIS, *puts his hand
on her shoulder, then heads for the door, right, followed by*
HEDDERLEY. MR. GODBOY *runs ahead, unlocks the door,
opens it for them.*)
(*Pauses by the guppie-case, looks in, wags his finger about,
looks at* MR. GODBOY, *who is holding the door open.*) I might
be back, Mr. Godboy, I might be back.

GODBOY (*looks at him*): I know that, Mannerly. I'll be ready.
(HAWKINS *tips his head, then goes out, followed by*
HEDDERLEY. MR. GODBOY *goes out of the room, after them.*)
(DORIS *looks towards the open door, right, then picks up the
stocking, which Hawkins has left on the sofa, picks up her
shoe and her handbag, tiptoes out into the kitchen left.*)
(*There is a silence on stage, then* DORIS *reappears through the
kitchen door, followed closely by* MR. GODBOY. *He escorts
her back to the chair, sits her in it.*)
There's the officer in a million for you, Doris. Inspector
Hawkins. Mannerly Hawkins. Did you notice his courtesy

74

in interrogation? The way he established that May Godboy was absent was a delightful piece of consummate skill. (*Looks down at her.*) But you're pale, my dear?

DORIS: What's he want then?

GODBOY (*after a pause*): He knows, Doris, and I know, but I can't tell you. It's between Mannerly and me. He's working in the dark but he'll get there in the end. (*Little pause.*) With him, cat and mouse is an art.

DORIS: What's he want with Eric then?

GODBOY (*laughs*): Eric's got no place in this, he wouldn't bother himself with an Eric.

DORIS: Oh. (*Little pause.*) He had his hand on my knee, like last night again.

GODBOY: A red herring, Doris, that's known as. He had his hand on my shoulder, twice. (*Laughs.*) Twice. (*Turns, goes to the alcove, comes back with the cylinder, locks the door, right, picks up the gasmask, walks purposefully back to DORIS.*)

DORIS: No, I changed my mind.

GODBOY (*looks at her*): It's too late for that, Doris. It's now or never.

(*Bends over her, again a short struggle, straightens. DORIS is in the gasmask, sitting hunched.*)

He knows me for what I am, Doris, that's his secret, and soon he'll have the mouse, which is me, in his paws, and two's a better catch for him than one.

(GODBOY *picks up the end of the tube, thrusts it under the gasmask, turns to the cylinder, wrestles with the knobs. As he is doing this, DORIS snatches the tube out. The gas comes out, holds it up. MR. GODBOY turns.*)

Manley. Manley. (*In a long whisper.*)

(*Goes to DORIS, puts his hand on her shoulder, bends over her, sees the pipe DORIS is holding, grabs hold of it, takes a deep breath to exclaim, and still holding the pipe, reels away, grabs at the cylinder, turns off the tap, then crashing around the chair, sways to the sofa, watched by DORIS, who gets anxiously to her feet.*)

(*Lights.*)

CURTAIN

## Scene 2

*A couple of hours later.*

*Lights on* MR. GODBOY, *sitting on the sofa, his head lolling. He appears to be asleep, his hands are pressed into his crotch. He leaps suddenly to his feet, sits down again, stares ahead, slumps forward, buries his face in his hands. There is a knock on the door. It opens tentatively.* ERIC *puts his head in, smiles at* MR. GODBOY, *sniffs, makes a face.* MR. GODBOY *stares slowly at him.*

ERIC: Hullo!

> (*Comes in, carrying a small pail, smiles at* MR. GODBOY *who is still staring at him. Goes over, puts the pail on the guppie table, turns, sniffs again, coughs, makes as if to say something, checks himself, smiles.*)
> Um, didn't you say she'd be done now then?
> (*There is a long silence.* MR. GODBOY *looks at the cylinder on the floor, looks back at* ERIC. *Gets to his feet, walks over to* ERIC *slowly. Puts a hand on his shoulder.*)
> (*Laughs nervously.*) Where is she then? Is she upstairs?

GODBOY: Eric, I regret to inform you that your wife has met with a fatal accident.

ERIC (*uncomprehending*): What?

GODBOY: She didn't suffer, sir, that must be the main consolation at a time like this. Her release was instantaneous.

ERIC (*worried, looks at him apprehensively*): Where's Dorrie?

GODBOY (*his shoulders jump, goes back, sits down. Puts a hand to his head*): My wound is playing me up something terrible.

ERIC (*coming over to him*): Where's Dorrie?

GODBOY: An old wound. Pre-war. My dad did it to me, in a game with his belt.

ERIC (*shouting*): Where's my Dorrie?

GODBOY (*shouting back*): Don't you shout at me, old boy. A Special Constable's a Special Constable. (*Pause.*) Righto?

ERIC (*whimpering*): Where's my Dorrie?

76

GODBOY: I keep telling you. She met with a fatal attack, mistake, I merely——

(ERIC *begins to shake his head from side to side.*)

Would you mind restraining yourself, my personal giddiness isn't helped by it.

(*As* ERIC *looks at him.*)

A great release must be your main consolation. Remember your manners.

(*Staggers to the window, opens it, sticks his head out, comes back, watched by* ERIC. *Goes to the guppie case, picks up the food package, shakes it over them pauses, then puts his hands into the water and bending down, splashes his face. Straightens. Turns.*)

ERIC: Where is she?

GODBOY: Whom!

ERIC: Dorrie!

GODBOY (*looks around, confused. Stares at* ERIC): I have reason to believe that she must be laid out in the kitchen.

(ERIC *turns, makes as if to run to the kitchen.* MR. GODBOY *seizes his arm, they grapple,* ERIC *falls to the floor.* MR. GODBOY *sits on top of him.*)

This is bound to be a time of stress for you. I've had experience of grief in happier days. Kindly stop bobbing up and down, Eric, you're on my wound.

ERIC: Please, please, I've got to see her.

GODBOY: Why?

ERIC: I got to, she's my Dorrie!

GODBOY: There's nothing to see, merely her remains.

ERIC: Let me see her! (*Bucking frantically.*)

GODBOY: This is irregular. She's liable to be in a state of undress.

ERIC (*stops, stares up at* MR. GODBOY): What you done to her?

GODBOY: Don't you attempt to incriminate me, boy.

(*There is a long pause.*)

How was your pictures, old boy?

ERIC: It was all right, it was good.

GODBOY: Can that story be checked out. (*Cunningly.*)

ERIC: What?

GODBOY: I'm in the clear on this Eric, you're not good enough to play cat and mouse with me. And I'll tell you why. I left May——

ERIC: May?

GODBOY: Doris I merely mean, alone in the cupboard——

ERIC: Cupboard?

GODBOY: Kitchen I merely mean, don't keep confusing me, Eric it's a cheap trick, left her alone in the kitchen when compelled to fetch an emergency refill of my prescription. When I came back, I found her already passed away on the kitchen table and a moment later, although myself laid low by my wound, heard you hammering at the door in a state. (*Little pause, cunningly.*) You are in a state, aren't you? We can agree on that?

ERIC: Let me go to her, please.

GODBOY (*after a pause, gets up*): All right, Eric, I give you permission. I'm inclined to believe your story, but I'm not sure that a superior officer like Mannerly Hawkins would take a favourable view.

(*Shouting the last part of this after* ERIC, *who has run into the kitchen. Then goes to the sofa, sits down. Noises come from the kitchen.* MR. GODBOY *folds his hands into his lap, stares straight ahead. After a moment* ERIC *comes out, stares at him.*)

I've been thinking, Eric, it would look strange to the police if your wife was found dead in my kitchen. Kindly carry her upstairs, to your own parlour, where she belongs.

(*As* ERIC *sits down, as if in shock.*)

While you're about it please remove that cupboard I went to great annoyance to purchase for you. The ideal solution would be for you to cram May——

ERIC (*listlessly*): Doris.

GODBOY (*after a slight pause*): Doris, into the sea-trunk I noted among your possessions. It would be best for your own sake if you could get her in completely, try not to have anything hanging over the edge, then hoist the sea-trunk on top of May——

ERIC: Doris.

GODBOY: Nonsense, old boy, you can scarcely hoist Doris in

78

the cupboard on top of herself in the cupboard, can you? (*Laughs.*) It's May that's in the cupboard.

(ERIC *looks at him.*)

It's May's cupboard, I merely mean, Eric, old boy. So you hoist (*pause*) Doris in the sea chest on top of (*thinks*) the cupboard and then there'll be real cat and mouse with Mannerly when he comes calling. Those are my plans for you, I've thought them all out.

(ERIC *continues to stare at him.*)

Now (*rubs his hands together.*) Did you get her garments?

(ERIC *shakes his head.*)

What did you make of (*thinks*) Doris's (*nods*) appearance? (*Looks at* ERIC.) Did she look serene?

(ERIC *shakes his head.*)

(*Stares at him.*) Now, Eric, violence to a living creature——

ERIC: She isn't there.

(GODBOY *stares at him.*)

She isn't. No. . . . (*Shakes his head.*)

GODBOY: Where is she then?

ERIC: I don't know.

GODBOY (*gets up, goes into the kitchen, comes out again, carrying the gasmask*): Something's wrong here, old boy. You looked in the larder, did you? (*Half turning.*)

ERIC: She isn't there.

(*Pause, as* MR. GODBOY *stands uncertainly.*)

Now you tell me, you tell me (*slowly, raises a finger menacingly*), you tell me where my Dorrie is. (*Gets up, goes over, puts his finger close to* MR. GODBOY'*s face.*)

GODBOY (*walks past him, to the door, right, opens it, puts his head out, freezes as steps*): Good evening, sir, this is an honour, although to tell you the truth I was just off for another of my refills. Prescription for my gamey. . . .

(*Backs in, followed by* HEDDERLEY. *As he does so,* ERIC *backs out, in the kitchen, nearly closing the door.*)

(GODBOY *enters, followed by* HEDDERLEY. *They stand facing each other. There is a long pause.* MR. GODBOY'*s shoulders jump. He chuckles.* HEDDERLEY *stares unblinkingly. Little pause.* HEDDERLEY *sniffs.*)

A minor accident with some gassed cabbage-heads. Boiled over I merely—Mannerly not with you then?

HEDDERLEY: Soon.

GODBOY: That's very kind of him.

HEDDERLEY: I'm looking for Eric Hoyden.

GODBOY: Indeed?

HEDDERLEY: He's not upstairs.

GODBOY: That's his story. Can it be checked out? (*In a low voice.*)

HEDDERLEY: I'm not empowered to force an entry. (*Little pause.*) Is there anything you can tell me about him?

GODBOY: He's a fine lad (*lowering voice slightly*), in spite of a mild history of violence.

HEDDERLEY (*takes out note-book, jots down. Then goes to one of the utility chairs, crosses legs, skirt slightly hiked, left stocking rumpled*): Yes?

GODBOY: It's not his fault he doesn't know his own strength. To look at he's a reed, so if other people don't know his strength, and he's not so quick frankly (*taps his forehead*) as other people, how can *he* know it.

HEDDERLEY: Yes? (*Writing.*)

GODBOY: Nothing is known against him in this house except his fondness for gas which he can't keep from talking about. (*Pause.*) In his quiet moments he's deceptively likeable.

HEDDERLEY (*writes*): Yes?

GODBOY (*coming closer*): His word's not to be trusted (*in a low voice, then stepping casually away*), he's got a wonderful sense of humour.

HEDDERLEY (*writing*): Yes?

GODBOY (*as* ERIC's *face appears around the kitchen door, sees it*): I'll stand by Eric to the end. If you need a character witness, don't hesitate to call on me to speak out.
(ERIC *shuts the door.*)
He can't help his habits, they're second nature.

HEDDERLEY: Yes? (*Writing.*)

GODBOY: You're conducting this investigation very quietly and firmly, officer, and I'll be glad to report that to Mannerly. (HEDDERLEY *stares at him, then puts the note-book away. Keeps staring at him.*)

80

The last I saw of Eric (*coming closer*), he was off after his
May. Doris. (*Little pause.*) What is the precise nature of
the charges being laid against him?

HEDDERLEY: That depends on what he's done.

GODBOY: There's British Justice for you (*as* HEDDERLEY *re-
crosses legs.*)

HEDDERLEY: Where's your wife? (*Quickly.*)

GODBOY: Still away sir. (*Quickly.*)

HEDDERLEY (*after a pause*): Why do you call me sir?

GODBOY (*laughs, shakes his head*): Pardon.

HEDDERLEY: When do you expect him back?

GODBOY (*quickly*): When she's rested.

HEDDERLEY: Who's rested? (*Quickly.*)

GODBOY: Doris . . . May. (*Quickly.*)

HEDDERLEY (*quietly*): I was asking you about Eric Hoyden.
(*Gets up, takes a step towards him. Stocking slipping.*)
Where is he?

GODBOY: Well, Eric's a law in himself. (*Shakes his head.*) I must
say I don't know why I confused Doris and Eric like that,
they're quite different kettles of fish (*laughs*) naturally.

HEDDERLEY: Your wife Doris?

GODBOY: Doris Godboy, my wife.
(*Nods, begins to rock back and forth, sees that* HEDDERLEY'
*stocking is slipping. Stares as* HEDDERLEY *flicks through the
pages of the note-book, then stops.*)
No indeed. May. (*Slaps his forehead.*) May Godboy. Eric
is Doris's wife.
(*The kitchen door opens softly and* ERIC *puts his head in.*)

HEDDERLEY (*steps very close to* MR. GODBOY): Why are you
staring at me?
(*As* MR. GODBOY *begins to shake his head.*)
I need to adjust my clothing.

GODBOY: Pardon?

HEDDERLEY (*as the door opens wider, throws her leg out, hoists up
skirt.* MR. GODBOY *stares, turns hurriedly, folds his arms*):
Kindly turn around, we're not permitted to interrogate
from behind.
(*GODBOY turns slowly, stares straight ahead, a fixed smile*

*on his face.*)

(HEDDERLEY *fiddles with suspender clip, then very sharply.*)
Where is your wife?

GODBOY: Purley.

HEDDERLEY: We may need her to testify. Where can she be reached?

GODBOY: Thatch Cottage, Mimosa Drive.

(ERIC *is staring transfixed at* HEDDERLEY's *leg. Takes a step inside.*)
Failing that the Y.W.C.A. If she can't get into her Auntie's house, she stays at the Y.W. They're very tolerant there.

(ERIC, *his mouth hanging open, shuffles another step forward, begins to shake his head.*)
Failing that she may have gone to one of her other aunties. She likes to go from auntie to auntie indiscriminate.

(HEDDERLEY *stands, as* ERIC *is about to shuffle forward again.* ERIC *turns, goes quickly back out of the kitchen.*)

(*There is a long pause.* HEDDERLEY *and* MR. GODBOY *stare at each other.*)

(*Clears his throat*): Does Mannerly use you often?

HEDDERLEY: Often.

GODBOY (*after another pause*): How did you come to enter the force, may I ask?

HEDDERLEY: Inspector Hawkins picked me out during a certain period when I was frequenting coffee bars in the Notting Hill area. He took me in hand, dealt with me like a Dutch Uncle, and then when he'd finished showing me the ropes invited me to apply for special duties.

GODBOY: He's got greatness in him.

HEDDERLEY (*stares at him, walks past to the door. Turns, smiles at* MR. GODBOY): What is your own attitude to violence?

GODBOY: I'm against some of it.

HEDDERLEY: Are you against discipline?

GODBOY (*after a pause*): It's not in my nature to hurt a living creature.

(*Little pause, as* HEDDERLEY *continues to smile at him.*)
Although my own sister used to apply it to me sometimes, when I was little. (*Stares at* HEDDERLEY *as if transfixed.*)

82

She used to compel me to roll down my trousers and she spanked me on my bare bottie. (*Laughs.*) She was only a few years older than me, but very strong. She wanted to join the force also. Unfortunately she fell victim to an unsavoury incident and had to leave for Dublin after the war. (*Long pause.*) She was like you in major respects.

HEDDERLEY (*nods*): Inspector Hawkins is for discipline. We'll be back later.

GODBOY: Thank you, sir.

(HEDDERLEY *looks at him, goes out, shuts the door. There is a long pause.* MR. GODBOY *stands staring at the door, as if in a trance.*)

(ERIC *comes in left, goes up to* MR. GODBOY, *tugs at his sleeve.*)

What do *you* want?

ERIC: I want my Dorrie.

GODBOY (*blinking, shakes his head*): Do you, old boy, well I can't help you in that. All I know is that something funny's going on with regards to you as far as the police are involved. Things keep turning black for you.

ERIC: What?

GODBOY: They seem to be after you in connection with May. May Godboy.

ERIC: Well, I don't know about May, it's Dorrie——

GODBOY (*laughs smoothly*): Eric, Doris is old enough to look after herself, if indeed she's alive. It's May the police are calling in my help for. Cat and mouse is warming up, Eric.

ERIC (*shakes his head*): It's my Dorrie——

GODBOY: Now, Eric, if you've anything you wish to clear off your chest in respect to the gassing of May Godboy, tell me now.

ERIC: What gassing?

GODBOY: Where's her remains, Eric?

ERIC: What remains?

GODBOY (*points dramatically at the cupboard*): Remains of May Godboy.

ERIC: You said she was in Purley, I heard you.

GODBOY: Then as long as Mannerly and I can find her there

83

(*walks away from* ERIC) there's nothing for you to worry about, is there? (*Whips around.*) What did you do this afternoon?

ERIC: I told you, I went to Virgin Mayo and Burt Lancaster.

GODBOY: Cinema alibis can be broken into shreds, Eric. Who's your witnesses?

ERIC: I—I—(*points to the pail*) I got you those. Them gups!

GODBOY: Was Doris with you at the time?

ERIC: She was with you.

GODBOY: Oh, and was she here when you got back, Eric?

ERIC: No, that's what I'm——

GODBOY: Who's your witnesses, Eric?

ERIC (*thinks*): You are. (*Nods.*)

GODBOY: Indeed? All I know is that I was laid out on account of my old wound and when I came to myself *you* was hammering about with loose questions of May having died in an accident. So who's your witnesses, Eric?

ERIC: Doris.

GODBOY: Hah. Hah hah. So it was *Doris* is dead.

ERIC (*shaking his head*): No, no, what I mean is May——

GODBOY: May!

ERIC: I haven't seen her.

GODBOY (*puts his face forward, hisses*): Witnesses, Eric, witnesses you need a witness, Eric, who's your witness, Eric, who? Who? (*Following him across the room as he backs away.*) (*The door right opens and* HAWKINS *steps into the room.*) (*Whipping around.*) Good afternoon, Mannerly, I was hoping you'd turn up, here's a real problem for you. (ERIC *makes for the kitchen door, opens it, a figure in blue is fleetingly visible. Closes the door, turns, faces the wall, left.*)

HAWKINS (*revolving his hat, walks towards* ERIC): Good afternoon, sir, I don't think I've had the pleasure. (ERIC *coughs.*)

GODBOY: Eric Hoyden, Inspector Hawkins is inquiring politely after your name.

ERIC: Eric Hoyden.

HAWKINS: Well, I'll say this for you, you're a difficult man to

put a hand on, Eric Hoyden.
(*Puts his hand on* ERIC'*s shoulder, turns him around slowly.*
ERIC *stands with his hands sunk into his pockets, head
lowered.*)
And what do you know about all this, sir?

ERIC: What?

HAWKINS: And now what does *what* mean, sir, may I ask. (*Puts
a finger under* ERIC'*s chin and lifts it up.*) What's *what*
mean, sir?

ERIC: Nothing.

HAWKINS: Is it nothing, then, sir? You've no burglaries to tell
me about? (*Gives* ERIC'*s jaw a little shake.*) No murders,
sir? (*Gives* ERIC'*s jaw a little shake.*) No (*little pause*)
indecent-assaults-and-handbag-snatching to turn my ears
with, sir?
(ERIC *attempts to shake his head.* HAWKINS *holds it steady.*)

ERIC (*pointing a finger at* MR. GODBOY, *who is standing with his
hands behind his back*): He—he—he done something to my
Dorrie, he did.

HAWKINS (*still holding* ERIC'*s jaw*): And have you done something to *his* (*slight stress*) Dorrie, Mr Godboy?

GODBOY: I wouldn't touch her with a barge-pole, Mannerly.
(*Laughs.* HAWKINS *turns his head, looks at him.*)
I've got too much respect, sir.

ERIC: He did, he did, he told me himself she was dead.

HAWKINS (*removes his hand from* ERIC'*s jaw, pats both his cheeks
simultaneously*): Well, sir, I can see you've nothing to fear
from the law, and certainly you wouldn't mind a little
inspection from one of my men. (*Little pause. Shouts.*)
Hedderley!
(*Whipping* ERIC *around to face the kitchen door as he does
so. The kitchen door opens simultaneously*, HEDDERLEY
*comes in.*)
(HEDDERLEY *walks slowly towards* ERIC. HAWKINS *moves
away to stand next to* MR. GODBOY. ERIC *stands transfixed.*
HEDDERLEY *stands facing* ERIC, *then puts arms about his
shoulders in a hug, sways about with him.*)

ERIC: Here! Here!

(HEDDERLEY *takes* ERIC'*s hand and presses it against her right leg, moves it up under the skirt.*)
Here! (*Bending over.*)
(HEDDERLEY, *straightens, drops* ERIC'*s hand, turns, nods once to* HAWKINS. HAWKINS *beckons with his head.*
HEDDERLEY *goes to him, they walk to the other end of the room, whispering.*)
(ERIC *looks towards them, makes for the kitchen door, left.*)
HAWKINS (*without turning*): Would you be kind enough to hang on a little, sir, thank you, sir.
(ERIC *stops.*)
(GODBOY *looks towards* HAWKINS *and* HEDDERLEY, *goes over, takes* ERIC'*s arm.*)
HAWKINS (*turns*): Now that's a lovely pair of trousers.
(ERIC *looks down at his trousers, looks away.*)
(HAWKINS *whispers to* HEDDERLEY. GODBOY *fingers* ERIC'*s trousers.*)
(*Turning.*) Would you do Constable Hedderley the kindness of permitting Constable Hedderley the use of your toilet?
GODBOY: Indeed, Mannerly, it's across the hall, Hedderley.
HAWKINS (*staring at* ERIC, *repeats*): Would you do Constable Hedderley the kindness of permitting Constable Hedderley the use of your toilet?
ERIC (*after a silence*): What?
HAWKINS: Your toilet, sir. Constable Hedderley's in trouble.
ERIC: Oh. (*As* HEDDERLEY *comes towards him.*)
HAWKINS: Oh now, sir, you wouldn't be one of those citizens who demands a search warrant from an officer desperate for a toilet, sir, would you?
ERIC: Um . . . all right.
(HEDDERLEY *holds out a hand.*)
HAWKINS: Now where exactly did you say your toilet was, sir?
ERIC: Upstairs landing.
HAWKINS: Now there's great stress in the force on personal hygiene, Constable Hedderley will be wanting to wash her hands in your sink afterwards, could you let her have the keys to get in with, sir?
ERIC (*after a pause*): I lost them.

(GODBOY *puts his hand into* ERIC'*s trouser pocket, takes out the keys, holds them triumphantly to* HEDDERLEY. HEDDERLEY *stares at them.*)

HAWKINS: Mr. Godboy, I think those are Mr. Hoyden's keys, and I advise you to return them to him immediately, Mr. Godboy.

(GODBOY *looks towards* HAWKINS, *gives the keys to* ERIC. HEDDERLEY *takes them from* ERIC.)

Manners, Hedderley!

HEDDERLEY: Thank you, sir. (*To* ERIC. *Goes out.*)

(*There is a silence.* HAWKINS *stands rotating his hat, smiling at* ERIC. MR. GODBOY *stands bewildered, looking from* HAWKINS *to* ERIC. ERIC *stands hunched.*)

HAWKINS (*to* ERIC): Now I think, sir, you were saying something about *your* (*slight stress*) Dorrie, I think.

ERIC: He knows, he knows. (*Nods at* MR. GODBOY.)

(*There is the sound of an upstairs lavatory flushing. They all stare up at the ceiling. There are crashing sounds from above.*)

HAWKINS: Well, if anything's happened to that young lady, there'd be some answering would have to be done, to the law and to myself. (*Little pause.*) There was a young lady once, permitting herself to be humbly searched down at the station when she was innocent of everything but weakness of spirit, and I caught a glimpse of her through a crack in the door when she was standing with only her little hands for covering, and then I was called off to a breaking and entering and when I got back she was lost to me. Now I've been looking for that young lady——

(*The door, right, opens.* HAWKINS *and* MR. GODBOY *turn towards it.* ERIC *stares quickly away as* HEDDERLEY *comes in carrying arm-loads of handbags and a pair of trousers.* HAWKINS *and* MR. GODBOY *go on staring, as the door left, opens,* DORIS *puts her head in,* ERIC *sees her, takes a step towards her.* DORIS *looks around the room, sees* HAWKINS *shuts the door.*)

ERIC: She's—she's——

(ERIC *turns, sees the handbags and trousers, stops. There is a long silence on stage.* HEDDERLEY *drops the handbags, comes towards* HAWKINS, *hands him the trousers.* ERIC *turns around again.* HAWKINS *takes the trousers, shakes them out. They have a large section missing at the fly.*)

HAWKINS (*strides across to* ERIC, *turns him around, takes his chin in his hand.*) So now we know what you do between jobs, Between-Jobs Eric. You do the ladies of Merrit Street, sir. (*There is a long silence.*)

GODBOY: You mean there were *two* Merrit Street attackers, Mannerly?

HAWKINS: Just one lucky one (*turns* ERIC'*s face to the right, then to the left*) who must be thanking God (*turns* ERIC'*s face up to the ceiling*) he's been taken at last. (*Releases him.*) We should have had you last night, Between-Jobs, all the misery of your guilt should have been over for you in the darkness of last night, if Constable Hedderley hadn't over-baited himself with heavy perfume and a skirt too tight it prevented him from running free. Isn't that so, Hedderley?

HEDDERLEY: Sir.

HAWKINS: Ah, while Constable Hedderley, coated in this perfume and hobbled at the legs, was throwing Between-Jobs around on the pavement, the dogs, unable to recognize Hedderley's natural body-odours, sprang straight at Constable Hedderley. Except, that is, for an elderly bitch with dirty habits who plunged straight for Between-Jobs, preferring the male smell of *him*, and tore this (*little pause, takes out of his pocket the cloth from* ERIC'*s trousers, complete with fly-buttons, and holds it against the torn trousers*) from the Merrit Street attacker. So (*to* ERIC) another day you had to suffer through, for your release.

GODBOY: And to think I left you alone in my kitchen with May!

ERIC: I wasn't going to—I wasn't going to—I'd made myself stop doing it. But she (*looks at* HEDDERLEY) he—she—was pulling her stockings up and smiling at me and winking and my head was buzzing from May's stout and gin, and I just meant to help out with something and the next minute she was whirling me about and holding me on the ground and his knee was in my back and her arm was around my throat and there was these dogs, these dogs. . . . (*Covers his face with his arm.*)

(*Long silence.*)

HAWKINS: There, there, boy, it's all right. It's all over for you now. (*Little pause.*) Or will be when you tell us where our Dorrie is.

ERIC: She's in the kitchen.

GODBOY: Don't tell lies, Eric, it won't serve. You took her away somewhere this afternoon and gassed her or something like that, and we both know it.

HAWKINS (*takes a step towards* ERIC, *restrains himself*): Just tell us, son, and then we can have a good talk about the other matter down at the station.

ERIC: She was here, he done it, I don't know, she's—(*stops, looks at the faces*) I tell you.

(HAWKINS *looks at* HEDDERLEY, *turns, walks to the front of the stage.*)

(HEDDERLEY *takes* ERIC'*s arm, and leads him to the sofa, makes him sit down, bends over him.* MR. GODBOY *stands somewhere between* HAWKINS *and* HEDDERLEY, *his hands behind his back.*)

HAWKINS (*turns his head to* MR. GODBOY): When I was a little boy, Mr. Godboy, over there in County Mayo——

(GODBOY *nods attentively.*)

I had a dream of devotion, a lonely life given up to salvation. I dreamt that as a boy, I did.

(HEDDERLEY *bends over* ERIC, *does something to him,* ERIC *cries out.*)

(MR. GODBOY *turns his head, looks towards the sofa.*)

And come Sundays there was a special pond I'd walk to, deep and calm it was, and there in the long afternoon I'd sit and think of what was open to me to be done——

(HEDDERLEY *makes* ERIC *cry out again.* GODBOY *again looks towards the sofa, takes a step back to it.*)

And of the little I have to give. And my dog whiskers up to some doggy mischief at my feet or behind me in the bushes. (*Shakes his head, smiling.*)

(HEDDERLEY *makes* ERIC *cry out again.* GODBOY *takes*

*another step back.*)

And somehow in those days the sun was always shining, yes it was, or that's the way I see it now, from the black heart of the big city. When I look back to it from no more Sundays in Mayo.

(GODBOY *who has been standing, looking down at* ERIC, *his hands behind his back, watches* HEDDERLEY *bend over* ERIC *again.*)

And yet somewhere in the back of my mind is the picture, I'll keep it there through disciplining and pain, of what it is I've lost.

(GODBOY *leans over and does something experimental to* ERIC. *Then* HEDDERLEY *does it. Then* ERIC. *In a see-saw rhythm.*)

ERIC (*screaming out*): I tell you she was there, larking about in the kitchen.

GODBOY: I won't have you telling lies about my kitchen, Between-Jobs.

HAWKINS (*smiling*): Through disciplining and pain I hug it to me, that Sunday afternoon when I dreamed of devotion, by an eternal pond, in an eternal sunshine, and I——

(DORIS *puts her head around the kitchen door, stares at the scene on the couch, takes a few frantic steps in, stops.* HEDDERLEY *and* GODBOY *go on working on* ERIC.)

(*Turns, sees* DORIS.) —am boy eternal.

(*Goes over to* DORIS, *takes her gently by the arm, leads her to the centre of the stage.*)

GODBOY: Where is she, Between-Jobs, where is she, where?

HEDDERLEY: Where? Where?

(*They bend simultaneously over him.*)

HAWKINS (*puts a finger under* DORIS'*s chin, tilts her face up*): And I am boy eternal, Doris. I thought you'd been taken from us (*very gently*), where have you been, Doris?

(ERIC *lets out a long shout.* HAWKINS *looks towards them as* GODBOY *turns his face around. He is laughing, sees* DORIS, *nods to her, turns back to* ERIC. *Begins to do something, suddenly stops.* HEDDERLEY *stops.*)

Hedderley. (*Nods to the kitchen door.*)

90

(HEDDERLEY *helps* ERIC *from the sofa, takes him into the kitchen.*)

Mr. Godboy (*nods again to the kitchen door.*)

(GODBOY *hesitates, looks at* DORIS, *follows* HEDDERLEY.)

And Hedderley, there's to be only gentleness now, Hedderley.

HEDDERLEY: Sir.

HAWKINS: Mr. Godboy?

GODBOY: Sir.

(*They go into the kitchen, shut the door.*)

(HAWKINS *stands looking at* DORIS, *who clutches her handbag to her stomach, stares at the ground. There is a long pause. Then* HAWKINS *puts his hand through* DORIS's *arm, leads her to one of the utility chairs, sits her on it.* DORIS's *handbag drops from her lap, its contents scatter over the floor. She makes a move to pick it up.* HAWKINS *restrains her, pats her knee, crouches at her feet, begins to put her things back into the handbag.*)

HAWKINS: Are you frightened?

(DORIS *sits hunched.*)

Of course you are. I think it's part of your nature isn't it? (*Pause.*) Isn't it?

(DORIS *nods.*)

(*Shuts her handbag firmly, puts it back in her lap, stays on his knees*): And why has Eric been out in Merrit Street, grabbing at the ladies and their handbags then? (*Crooningly.*) Is it because you wouldn't let him near you, is it because he didn't know how to come near you, is it because you're frightened, Doris?

DORIS (*after a pause*): He didn't mean it. Not Eric.

HAWKINS (*strokes her foot*): Is he any good to you, Doris? (*Little pause.*) And is he, now? (*Takes her shoe off.*)

DORIS (*after a pause*): Don't know.

HAWKINS: And what good are you, Doris, all by yourself while Eric's away from us all? Will you get yourself taken away again by another Eric, poor Eric. Will you?

(DORIS *shrugs into a hunch.*)

What do you want, then Doris?

91

DORIS: Don't know.

HAWKINS: And who knows what you're wanting, Doris? (*Stands up slowly, stands over her, looks down.*) Who?

DORIS (*after a long pause, lifts her face to his. Pause.*) You? (*Whispered.*)

HAWKINS: And who'll make you a good girl, Doris?

DORIS: You.

HAWKINS: And who did I get a glimpse at, once, down at the station, and nude?

DORIS (*staring up*): Me. (*Whispered.*)

HAWKINS (*bends down, kisses* DORIS *on the mouth. Raises her up by the arms, kisses her again, passionately*): So what do you want, then, Doris?

(DORIS *staring into his face, whispers something inaudible.*)

(*Releases her slowly, looks at her.*) Hah! (*Slaps her playfully on the rump.*) Hah! Hedderley!

(*The kitchen door opens.* GODBOY *enters, stands aside with his hands behind his back as* ERIC *enters,* HEDDERLEY *holding his arm up behind him.*)

ERIC: Dorrie, Dorrie, you all right Dorrie?

(DORIS *looks down, her handbag clasped to her stomach again.*)

(HAWKINS *nods to* HEDDERLEY. ERIC *is released, stands upright.*)

HAWKINS: Are you all right, Doris?

(DORIS *looks at him, nods.*)

ERIC: I couldn't help it, Dorrie, I couldn't, it's 'cause I love you, Dorrie.

HAWKINS: Well, Doris, I think he's expecting an answer, have you got an answer for him?

(DORIS *looks at* HAWKINS, *shakes her head.*)

There's no answer for you, son. (*Goes to* ERIC.) You were going to come to me in the end, you see, and you'll be glad of it, in the end, you see. (*Little pause.*) Think of it, while you were slipping through my net I was sitting here, beneath your home, waiting for you without either of us knowing it. Something called me here, it was your own cry that called me here, son, and that's why I came. There's always a reason for accidents. The reason was that you were waiting for me, what else could it have been? Think of that.

GODBOY (*coughs, he has been standing restlessly during* HAWKIN'*s speech*): There could be other reasons, Mannerly, you could have come because someone——

ERIC (*swings up an arm, points his finger at* GODBOY, *stares at him*): It was you, you. (*There is a long silence, then cries out as if in revelation.*) He done for May!
(*Another silence. They look at* GODBOY, *who puts his hands behind his back, swells his chest.*)

GODBOY: That's who it's been between, Mannerly, all along. Cat and (*takes a step forward*) mouse.

ERIC (*nodding*): He done for May!

GODBOY: Where do you think she's concealed then?
(*Smiling at* HAWKINS, *who is looking at* ERIC.)
All along?

ERIC (*draws a deep breath, bursts out*): In the cupboard! In the cupboard, what's full of gas!

GODBOY: Mannerly? (*Smiling at him.*)

ERIC: That's it, the cupboard!

GODBOY: Quiet, rapist, people like you is two a penny now-a-days.

HAWKINS (*goes to* DORIS, *takes a hair-pin out of her hair, then as* ERIC *takes a step forward, without turning around*):
Hedderley.
(HEDDERLEY *takes* ERIC'*s arm again.* HAWKINS *goes over to the cupboard, bends down, fiddles the hair-pin into the lock.* GODBOY *turns, smiles at* ERIC *disdainfully, walks across to* HAWKINS, *stands beside him.*)

GODBOY: I want to say, Manly, you've cracked open something big here, that'll be a feather in your cap in all the newspapers. I've waited for you to show up here, waited and waited, and you did, Mannerly, just on time. Our turn together was doomed. Cat and mouse Mannerly, as you said yourself, the big mouse is in your paws at last.
(*As the lock clicks and* HAWKINS *stands upright.*)
Permit me, Mannerly, it's all I ask now the moment is come (*takes the door*), here is what you've been waiting

93

for, here is what was calling out to you.

(GODBOY *stands, stares* HAWKINS *in the face, then flings the door open.* HAWKINS *stares inside, then comes back to* DORIS, *nods to* HEDDERLEY. HEDDERLEY *pushes* ERIC *across the room past* GODBOY *who is staring blankly into the cupboard.* HAWKINS *follows, one hand resting carelessly on* DORIS's *rump. She is limping, clutching her handbag tight.* ERIC *suddenly breaks free of* HEDDERLEY, *and plunges into the cupboard, comes out again holds up his raincoat, shows it to* DORIS.)

ERIC: I said it was in there, didn't I, Dorrie?

(*Struggles defiantly into it.* HEDDERLEY *takes his arm, they go out.*)

HAWKINS (*to* GODBOY): There's a lot of confessing to be made. And don't worry yourself about Doris, what she needs is only a Dutch Uncle talking to. (*Looks at* DORIS.) I'll be showing you the ropes myself, Doris. (*Puts his hat on.*) Good-bye, Mr. Godboy, good-bye.

(*Replaces his hand on* DORIS's *rump. They go out.*)

(GODBOY *stands alone, staring after them. Then goes and sits down on the sofa. Sits staring ahead. A long wait. Then he gets up, goes forlornly over to the guppie case, is about to shake some food in, checks himself, picks up the pail, goes off stage, right. There is a pause.*)

(MAY *appears through the kitchen door, carrying her bags. Drops them on the floor, takes off her coat, drops it on the sofa, looks about her, goes back into the kitchen. Sound of a lavatory flushing.* GODBOY *comes in, puts the guppie case on the table, pours the guppies from the pail into it, scatters the food. Stands for a moment, back to the audience, then turns, looks at the cupboard, goes to it, stares in, steps in completely.* MAY *comes out of the kitchen door, smoking a cigarette, looks about her, then walks across the room towards the door, right, passing the cupboard. As she does so she slams the cupboard door shut, goes on out of the room, tapping ash.*)